DEAD BODIES & BROTHELS

Plus3 Press
Denver, CO

A 'Salida Sam' Historical Book

DEAD BODIES & BROTHELS

*The History of Salida, Colorado
Volume 2: 1882 & 1883*

Steven T. Chapman

Dead Bodies & Brothels
The History of Salida, Colorado, Volume 2: 1882 & 1883
Copyright © 2020 & 2022 Steven T. Chapman
All Rights Reserved
Printed in the United States by Plus3 Press
Second Edition

This book may not be reproduced, transmitted, or stored in whole or part by any means, including graphic, electronic, or mechanical without the express written consent of the author except in cases of brief quotations embodied in critical articles and reviews. For information, contact publisher or the author at StevenTChapman970@gmail.com.

All photographs are copyright protected by individual owners and used in this book with express written permission. Cover design by Joe Stone (joe@joestone.net).

ISBN: 9781655220913

Plus3 Press
Denver, CO

To be First to Learn About New Books in this Series, Visit:
www.SalidaWalkingTours.com/shop

PLUS3 PRESS
BOOKS BY STEVEN T. CHAPMAN

NONFICTION

LYNCHED! Mob Justice & A Madness for Blood—The Vigilante Murder That Stained Salida for Decades

MURDER! The Criminal Conspiracy & Coverup Behind the Slaying of Salida's Most Famous Marshal

Salida Burns Down: The History of Salida, Colorado, Volume 4: 1886-1887

Three Murdered Wives: The History of Salida, Colorado, Volume 3: 1884-1885

Dead Bodies & Brothels: The History of Salida, Colorado, Volume 2: 1882-1883

Blood, Booze & Whores: The History of Salida, Colorado, Volume 1: 1880 –1881

Break the Chains! How to Make Money Online, Work from Home & Profit While You Sleep

Home Watch: The Definitive Guide to Starting, Growing and Succeeding in the Vacation Home Care Industry

FICTION

The Hour of Noon

In Eddy We Trust

I Believe in You: Discussions with the Divine

TABLE OF CONTENTS

Acknowledgments

Author's Note

Forward

Sam Speaks

1882 Journals

    Chapter One: January 1882

    Chapter Two: February 1882

    Chapter Three: March 1882

    Chapter Four: April 1882

    Chapter Five: May 1882

    Chapter Six: June 1882

    Chapter Seven: July 1882

    Chapter Eight: August 1882

    Chapter Nine: September 1882

    Chapter Ten: October 1882

    Chapter Eleven: November 1882

    Chapter Twelve: December 1882

1883 Journals

    Chapter One: January 1883

    Chapter Two: February 1883

    Chapter Three: March 1883

Chapter Four: April 1883

Chapter Five: May 1883

Chapter Six: June 1883

Chapter Seven: July 1883

Chapter Eight: August 1883

Chapter Nine: September 1883

Chapter Ten: October 1883

Chapter Eleven: November 1883

Chapter Twelve: December 1883

1883 Insurance Maps of Salida

Key Dates in Salida History

Chronology of Key Salida Citizens

About The Author & About 'Salida Sam'

'Salida Sam' Historical Series

Bibliography

ACKNOWLEDGEMENTS

This book series doesn't exist without many writers and editors, most of whom passed away over a century ago.

While much of this series comes from endless hours spent reading books and articles (listed in the bibliography), the lion's share of the inspiration for the journal content of 'Salida Sam' Hayes comes from the archives of *The Mountain Mail, The Salida Mail,* and *The Salida Record.* For a historian, having access to first-hand accounts is invaluable.

Numerous newspapers served Salida over the years. Unfortunately, most folded quickly did not survive two devastating fires or were not saved.

To the reporters and editors who first observed and documented the moments described in this book, 'Thank you."

~Steve Chapman

AUTHOR'S NOTE

Please note that this book is Volume 2 of a series. If you prefer a linear story, begin with *Blood, Booze, and Whores: The History of Salida, Colorado—Volume 1.*

This book's facts, people, places, and dates are 100% accurate. Rather than a dull listing of specifics, I share Salida's fascinating history through a fictionalized journal. In it, I lean on a character channeled while acting as a guide for Salida Walking Tours (www.SalidaWalkingTours.com). His name is 'Salida Sam' Hayes. You'll often hear Sam's voice on our tours, mainly when I describe the true stories of Salida's colorful, often violent, beginnings.

A tour guide is part actor, part storyteller, and part creative spirit. 'Salida Sam' walked out of my imagination and onto the streets of modern-day Salida to help me bring history alive. It seemed only fitting to have him speak on these pages.

'Salida Sam' communicates with the rough-hewn voice of his era. He's from the 1800s, meaning he's not overly educated, is often crude and crass, and is not in sync with modern social and political sensibilities. He's a man of his time, and his time was frequently brutal, racist, and sexist.

This series focuses almost exclusively on happenings inside the city limits of Salida. There are already many wonderful books documenting the rail history, the story of Chaffee County, and specifics about various cultures that impacted the town. The 'Salida Sam' historical series is intentionally narrow and focused so readers can gain a deeper understanding of the particulars of Salida and why things developed in a specific matter. So, if it didn't happen in these constricted confines, you probably won't see it mentioned.

Although inspired by a man who never existed, 'Salida Sam' Hayes' log is 100% historically accurate, including dates, facts, and names. It results from hundreds (perhaps thousands) of hours of research. Dates are all exact within one week of the actual occurrence, as available research relating to the time is sometimes loose with specifics.

Volume 1 of this series, *Blood, Booze & Whores*, covered the first two years of this town, 1880 and 1881. Volume 2, *Dead Bodies & Brothels*, documents the years 1882 and 1883.

Few photographs exist of Salida before 1890. In this volume, where Salida photographs were unavailable, I included images from the nearby communities of Maysville, Garfield, and Granite. While these photographs are not 'local,' they are from the 1880s and accurately depict what a visitor could have expected in Salida.

Enjoy the continuing story of men and women seeking a home in this railroad boomtown. Their trues stories formed the foundation for what is now the quaint little city of Salida, Colorado.

~Steven T. Chapman, 2019

FORWARD

"Where do you get your stories?" That's the primary question from guests in my role as owner of Salida Walking Tours (www.SalidaWalkingTours.com). This business and our reputation for uncovering obscure historical facts and intriguing, true stories, often unknown even to long-time locals, seemed to appear out of nowhere in the summer of 2018. When answering the query about our fact-based tales, I typically state I'm a history nerd and have engaged in a years-long exploration of Salida history. That explanation is an accurate, if incomplete, account.

Here's the (fictionalized) rest of the story.

In 2012, while wandering an estate sale, I came across an old cedar chest. It was in terrible condition, destined for a landfill or conversion to kindling. Being curious, I lifted the lid and peered inside and noticed faded photographs and a dark brown volume with yellowed pages falling out. Assuming it was a ledger or an old notebook, I picked up the binding, blew off the dust, and opened it to a random section. It appeared to be a journal. Such things do not usually grab my attention, but I noticed the word 'Salida' on a few pages and started skimming the hand-written scribblings.

The first date I came across, January 1, 1881, intrigued me, so I flipped the pages and noticed other entries extending for decades.

The journal contained a storyteller's voice, jammed with details about people and places, so I assumed it was a long-forgotten manuscript. Another great American historical novel that never found a market. But I was intrigued. Tucking the fragile collection under my arm, I located the sales manager and asked what she wanted for the faded, ripped pages. Realizing I had no interest in pricey antiques and paintings, she turned her nose up and said, "Just take it."

That evening, I started at the journal's beginning and devoured every faded page. There was a person behind the words who sounded fascinating, genuine, and real. There were a lot of details in the sentences, too many for a good novel. The writer was a colorful character who seemed to have first-hand knowledge of his subject matter. His 'facts' about Salida seemed plausible even though I'd never heard or read most of the information. Soon after, I began researching the validity of the tales contained in this diary.

In the end, I confirmed that the stories in 'Salida Sam' Hayes' journal are rooted firmly in documented history. Every specific in these pages is verifiable through history books, newspapers, and interviews. You can look them up yourself.

The dates are accurate, the stories are correct, and the information is accurate. Sam probably made up the limited dialogue, a bit of creative license, I suppose, but who can say? I wasn't there. However, it appears that he was.

I've not changed one word of 'Salida Sam' Hayes's journals or corrected his grammar. However, I did tweak the spelling for readability, tossed in quotation marks and commas (Sam didn't use either), and added section separators and chapter divisions.

Where do I get stories for Salida Walking Tours? I borrow them from Sam's writings. His style is humorous, personable, sometimes angry and self-righteous, and often crude, but the man was an engaging storyteller.

So, here it is, transcribed and brought to life in the modern era— Volume 2 of 'Salida Sam' Hayes's accurate, fact-filled personal journal of the history of Salida.

~Steven T. Chapman

SAM SPEAKS
Start at the Start

I ain't no writer. Cain't turn no clever phrase nor write down words what might make a woman cry. I ain't no educated man. Never was rich nor some tycoon what changed the world. Hell-fire, a person might say I'm only a simple drunk. Wouldn't have no cause to shoot a feller over such words as they might not be all wrong. I figure a man ought to own up to what he is or what he ain't. No sense arguing over facts even if they hurt. That ain't nothing but wasted time.

Now I might of spruced up a detail or 3 when writing the true tales on this here bunch of papers. That's just being entertaining. But one particular of this book cain't no-one argue with. It happened. All of it. And I was there.

I started writing cause a city feller is paying me to. He's a dude thru and thru, but cash money talks. It sure beats working on the rail line or digging wells. That there's real work, don't matter who your pappy was. Ain't never been fond of sweating work. Seems if I worked so hard in the night-time putting liquids in my body, it'd be down-right wasteful to make it all come back out in the day.

This dude come from back East and spent a few nights drinking with me. He bought the liquor, so I talked to him. My momma ain't raised no fool. One night he says to me, "Hayes, you tell some tall tales. Biggest ones I ever heard."

"Mister, you calling me a liar?" I says back. Now, I don't know about where you been raised, but in these parts, you call a feller a liar, you best say it from the comfort of friends or a revolver.

I dropped a hand to my holster and prayed to the sweet Lord I misheard the dude. Ain't never shot a man my whole life, other than a few Injuns, they don't count no ways, but I been knowed to bend a few noses with my barrel. I always figured shooting a man meant looking over a shoulder forever, and that don't sound pleasing.

The dude he throws his hands up in the air and apologizes faster than a man stepping on the toes of a woman whose great big husband is watching. "No, sir," he shouts. "I mean, you are interesting. You got a way of talking what makes people wanna listen more. This place is about to be a genuine boom town. I want you to write about what happens here so we can sell your stories about life on the frontier to folks back East. That's all I meant."

I damn near wet my trousers on account of I ain't want to shoot the dude no more than he want to get shot. I don't think he had a handle on how people settle things out here. I laughed and says I'd tell him all the tales he wanted if'n he keep buying drinks. But the dude says he want 'em wrote with a pen and paper. Said for me to start some-thing called a *journal*. A wrote account of the hoots 'n hollers here-abouts. But only true stories what I lived or heard from those who lived 'em. For cash money.

This here were April 1880. Like I said, my momma ain't raised no fool. So here we be. Me writing about a town what started as a little sand bar on the edge of the Arkansas River, in the middle of the Colorado Territory, in a place called Lake County, and you reading it.

'Salida Sam' Hayes

Stoner, J. J, and Beck & Pauli. *Bird's eye view of Salida, Chaffee County, Colorado.* Madison, Wis, 1882.

JOURNALS
'Salida Sam' Hayes Journal
Volume 2

CHAPTER ONE
January 1882

January 2, 1882
A new year and more new folk in town with new businesses. Cheap John's Clothing, from New York City, got ém a place now, next to Dickman's lumber yard. More damned Yankees heading here it seem.

~

What the difference in a Yankee and a damned Yankee? A Yankee comes down for a visit and goes home. A damned Yankee comes down for a visit and stays.

~

Cheap seems to be the word around here. Cheap Charley's from St. Louis opened in Hallock's building. These new fellers ain't got one new thought betwixt them.

~

Crane and Brennon opened a saloon with free supper. That always catches the boys.

~

Levi Cook, from Chaffee City and Maysville, opened a restaurant on North First Street in one of Van Every's buildings.

~

A.M. Alger came down from Boston to open a drug store. Sits in Sweet's new building, opposite the post office. Still another damned Yankee.

~

Feller name W.B. McKinney came to open a daily new-spaper. *The Mountain Mail* fellers says better he try a daily than them. Theys sticking to a weekly.

January 3, 1882
Other than businesses, lots other growing going on. Craig brothers adding to their store so's they can carry Queensware and wallpaper.

~

Captain Blake thinking of opening a race track on his property next to town. He must be tired of hauling mail. Seems a tire-some job to me.

~

Some-one putting a frame building on Second Street, betwixt E and F, for a black-smith shop.

~

J.B. Thompson put a third chair in his barber-shop.

~

Charley Johnston, lunch counter feller what got a place at the end of the bridge, building a bigger place for a full business. The rail depot needs a good eating house.

~

Blake adding to the rear of his store with a front on F Street. 18 by 24 feet. Post office moving there.

January 4, 1882
A new year don't bring all good happenings. Vernon and Harris closed shop. W.A. Hawkins soon retiring as Justice of the Peace and Police Justice. Gonna just serve as Mayor. But he still judging. 2 girls of easy virtue got arrested Thursday and took before him for making a ruckus.

~

Black-smith shop at the round-house burned down. Folks thinking it were set on purpose.

~

Theys talk of getting a Odd Fellow's Lodge in town. Don't understand grabbing hold of such a name. Seems down-right odd.

~

J.B. Bowne elected police magistrate by the town board.

January 5, 1882
Big talk of building a county hospital here in town. Few dozen of the local big-wigs met at Presbyterian's church to figure what they gots to offer to the county board for it to come here. Lots of them rich fellers says they give up land to make it happen. Can't imagine having so much you land could give some away for free.

~

Town board went to King's ranch to check a spring. Says it will work fine for the water-works. Theys gonna dicker with King to use the water.

January 6, 1882
Max Dickman went to Park County. Rumor were he got married. Max says it ain't so.

~

The Mountain Mail damn near burnt down. If not for Mr. Mullenix seeing it happening, the whole place woulda gone up in smoke. Sparks got lodged in a drapery from a big ole fire burning in-side.

~

L.W. Craig took off on a business-man's trip to St. Louis, Texas, and points east and south. Gonna be gone 5-7 weeks.

January 7, 1882
Had us a bunch of races on a track near town Satur-day. One were a 100 yard foot race betwixt Billy Dunn and one other. Billy won. I ain't saying them boys run slow, but the total time didn't go over 2 minutes. Also had some 400-yard horse races which were fun to see.

~

A drunk were prowling around town the other night. Got booted out of French's drug store for trying to steal a hatchet.

January 8, 1882
The snow we missed in December caught up to us. Lordy, windy too! And cold? 15 below Monday. That there is cold for sure.

~

Children's got ém a new past-time. It called foot-ball. Theys playing day and night. Gonna throw that thing through a window soon enough, and that will be that or a whupping sure to follow.

~

Harry Haywood now running Lady Gay Saloon on the north end of town.

January 10, 1882
Joe Roosa back in town, making boots again. Set up shop on Front Street next to Hawkins Hotel. Wonder if he gonna be a might smarter about conning people this go around?

~

Them big wigs done it. County commissioners agreed Salida the best place for the county hospital. Few high rollers gave 8 acres to build on. Seems we beat out them boys in Buena Vista and Nathrop. Theys sure to start squawking when the news hits.

~

Captain Blake left for Kansas City. Not sure why.

January 13, 1882
Hartzell got lumber on the ground for a new building in back of his bank.

~

When that water-works gets built, gonna have us genuine fire hydrants on every main corner in town. Fancy we getting.

~

Mrs. Bender had another grand party Tuesday night. Champagne and other good liquors flowed. A good time were had by all.

~

DandRG says theys gonna build a switch on this side of the river. That will be dandy for those with heavy freight. Beats the hell outa trying to cross that sad bridge with a big load.

January 14, 1882

Had a terrible accident Wednesday evening by the depot. A lady died. Mrs. John D. Monroe, from Leadville, were on the DandRG train with her 2 little children. The train stopped in Salida like it always do, half-past 7 at night, for a 20 minute lay-over so's folks could grab dinner.

When the train stops for dinner, it goes along the station platform so's folks on board can get out easy enough. Then they puts on the sleeping car soon's every-one gets off the train. Train always backs down the siding for the sleeping car to get put on.

Them train fellers rang the bell and whistle as they do when reversing so's every-one knows. Then, Lord a'mighty, they was a shrieking the likes of which I ain't never heard.

What I seen gonna haunt me till I die my-self.

Mrs. Monroe were lying on the ground, screaming in wild pain.

The train fellers stopped the cars right away, and a bunch of us runned over to help the poor woman. We lifted her up to the station platform. Luck had it a surgeon were there, and he took over. Weren't much the doc could do.

Mrs. Monroe had her left leg cut off betwixt the knee and thigh. The doc found the artery to stop extra bleeding. We carried her into the waiting room. That's when we seen her right leg were broken below the knee. Poor woman stayed conscious the whole time. Even with her wild pain, she told her name and where she were from, and some-one sent a tele-graph to her husband in Leadville.

How such a terrible thing happen, we all wonder?

Few fellers standing on the platform says after all the passengers left the train and headed to the supper-room, a lady showed up on the platform of one of the coaches. This were just as the train started down to get the sleeper car. Mrs. Monroe stood for a second then made a jump for the platform. There were about 2 feet betwixt the car steps and the platform. She missed her aim on the jump. The wheels of the car rolled right over her left leg and cut it clean off. Smashed the other leg something fierce. Her shoe were found right there on the track.

Soon's he got the tele-graph, Mr. Monroe got on a special train the rail-road set up so's he could rush from Leadville to Salida. He pulled in around mid-night. Mrs. Monroe passed away about the same time.

January 16, 1882

Them fire man's got ém new caps and shirts. A stylish bunch they look. But I can't figured out what style got to do with putting out fire.

~

Weather let up enough for construction to start again. Town been dang quiet with the cold and the wind and the snow.

~

Lizzie Langdon's whore-house finally open and running. Ain't had time to get there yet, but I sure will soon enough.

~

Sunday night, feller knowed as 'Tid-bit from Gunnison' dressed his-self in ladies clothes at Lady Gay Saloon to have a little fun. We all laughed, but Marshal Stingley threatened to arrest him. Tid-bit begged so piteously for mercy the Marshal let him off with a warning. We all so busy laughing at the scene I damn near pissed my-self.

~

That Yankee feller, Alger from Boston, building his drug store and got goods coming in fast.

~

Miles Mix took over for A.T. Ryan as deputy sheriff. Seems Ryan had enough of drunks and fools. Don't know what took him so long to find the trail.

Venable's Hotel, Maysville, Colorado 1882
Donna Nevens Collection, Salida Regional Library, Salida, Colorado

January 17, 1882

Work moving fast on the new post office. Be open soon.

~

Gessert brothers new bakery and restaurant open. Gonna specialize in oysters. Some-thing I ain't never ate. Seems peculiar paying cash money to swallow some-thing so slimy.

~

Rail-road boys busy re-building the black-smith shop at the round-house. Says it gonna look better than before.

~

Girl at the Lady Gay Saloon got busted up bad by a man name Reddy what found his-self in the calaboose for the beating.

January 20, 1882

Tele-graph came to Deputy Sheriff Mix asking him to arrest a feller name Ruddle. It came from George Taylor at Marshall Pass, says Ruddle wanted for theft. Marshal Stingley arrested Ruddle about 7 Sunday night and tossed him in the calaboose, but come early morning Ruddle and a bunch others ain't there.

Also missing were a man from Buena Vista, name Dooley. He got his-self locked up for abusing his wife and calling her all

the vulgar names in the calendar. Then he got after her with a knife before the law got called.

About 5 in the morning, when Marshal Stingley were making final check on the calaboose before turning in for a few hours of rest after a long day and night, he sees the jail doors busted open wide and the prisoners all gone. That included Reddy, the one jugged for bruising that female friend of his at Lady Gay Saloon.

The Marshal figured Dooley headed home which were true. Dooley told Marshal Stingley that Reddy and Ruddle busted open the door by prying off the iron strips. Says they told him he gots to run with them and he did.

Reddy were found by the Marshal in bed at the Lady Gay Saloon and got tossed back in the calaboose. Ain't heard if he were in the bed of the girl he beat, but ain't no surprise if he were. Women ain't too bright when it comes to for-giving bad men.

Ruddle ain't got found, and theys thought he headed to Brown's Canyon to lay low. Wonder if he be found in a whore's bed too?

January 21, 1882

W.C. Richardson to build the new T. Cameron and Company building on F Street. It to be 20 by 50 feet, 1-story.

~

Work-men rushing to build the Opera House so's folks can have a proper meeting place.

~

Mr. Bacon accidentally shot his-self with a shot-gun but recovering. Dr. Brown says he took out 141 pieces of shot. Bacon a damn fool, but talented. Me, I ain't got arms long enough to shoot my-self with a shot-gun.

~

Tallman had some fine looking pigs in front of his meat market. 3 of them to-gether dressed at 1,225 pounds. That's a lot of bacon. Got raised by Judge Eubank of the Junction Hotel.

~

The husband of that woman what got killed under the rail-road car, feller name J.D. Monroe from Leadville, says he thinking of suing the DandRG for $50,000 for damages. What kind of god-damn non-sense that be? Women dumb enough to jump across the track in a dress and the rail-road in the wrong? I ain't no fan of the rail-road but that this ain't no-thing but stupidity and greed.

January 22, 1882
Doc says to get vaccinated against small-pox. Outbreaks all over the valley.

~

Seen a advertise-ment in the news-paper, likes of which I ain't never seen. A young lady says she gots a kitchen stove and a house and a lot and wants a husband. "Age and infirmity no objection, provided money comes with it." If that don't beat all. Whores took to advertising in the news-paper.

~

Swede girl name Bue died at Mr. Reeves House. She lived on charity while in the county. Coroner says she died of child-bed fever from a cold she took after birthing a baby. Ain't no one claiming her nor the baby. Seems the least the bastard what put her in the family way could do is pay up so's she could have a decent burial.

January 24, 1882
Another damned Yankee looking to set up shop in Salida. Big bunch of boot and shoe manufacturers what trade in Colorado, New Mexico, and Utah. Says they gonna bring others here from their company to look around. I says let ém look and head back East.

~

The big wheels in town about to get bigger. Webb, W.E. Robertson, Roller, and those Salida Mining and Milling Company boys to build a mill here to reduce low-grade ore from placer bars along the river. Gonna cost ém $10,000 and says to process 24 tons a day. Them boys gonna strip the sand right from the river.

January 27, 1882
Hotels all full day and night. Business good all-around in town.

~

That didn't take long. Cheap John's cheaped out and moved to Gunnison. Ain't that just like a Yankee?

~

Some in town wanting a military unit formed off as part of the National Guard. Ain't sure why. Got no Indians in these parts, and what little trouble happens gets took care of by the Sheriff or Marshal.

January 30, 1882

Theys talk amongst the business fellers of buying the Poncha hot springs and piping the water to town. Sounds like the same drunk talk I heard when Salida first became a town. Ain't no-thing but hot air.

~

Dickman's Opera House got framing of the second story up. Gonna be a fine place and looking to open soon.

~

A feller name Dr. Gibbons gonna give him a talk on not drinking, at the church Sunday night. Some-thing theys call temperance. Sounds more like temper-mental to me. Fool's talk. Fellers ain't gonna give up the liquor.

January 31, 1882

Theys digging out under West's new block, corner Second and F Street, for a cellar.

~

I heard a couple of youngsters talking the other day. Theys yapping about the 'bad place,' which I figure mean hell but it might mean church. One says, "Well, if Satan goes to abusing my mamma, I'll tell Baxter Stingley." That's a heap of faith to put in a law-man.

~

Folks must think theys a ton of gold in this river. Fellers starting them a stock company with 1 million shares for sale at $100 a share for placer ground 2-3 miles below town. That's a mighty big dream.

~

Mr. Wheeler gots a contract with Johnson and Chenoweth to build next to that new Opera House. Gonna cost him $2,500. I shoulda learnt to work as a carpenter. Wheeler must think it gonna make a big success as he gone over to Iowa to bring his family here. He also buying stock for a hardware store.

~

Still gots the sound of hammer and saws making music all the damn time. Looks like sleep ain't never again gonna be peaceful in this town.

CALL ON
CHEAP CHARLEY

For goods and new prices.

He is now ready to show you a larger assortment, to sell cheaper and to give you MORE GOODS for your money than any store in the Arkansas Valley. Willl guarantee every sale or refund the money.

COME ONE AND ALL

and examine goods before you buy goods elsewhere.

Hallock's Building, Salida, Colorado.

CALL ON
CHEAP JOHN

From New York City, Canon City, Rosita, Buena Vista, Poncha Springs, Silver Creek, Sargent, Gunnison City, Crested Butte and Salida, next to Dickmann's Lumber Yard.

DEALER IN
CLOTHING
And Gents Furnishing Goods.
MINERS' SHIRTS, BLANKETS, ETC., A SPECIALTY.
Cheaper than the Cheapest.

Advertisements from The Mountain Mail, 1882

CHAPTER TWO
February 1882

February 1, 1882
  Mr. and Mrs. Frank Seeley had a 8-pound baby boy.

~

  The Peaked Sisters putting on a show for town Tuesday.

~

  Got a ice house what took over the place of McIntire and Bean's warehouse. Seems them fellers built it on rail-road property, thought to be owned by Van Every. The rail-road told ém to tear it down cuz it were too near the depot. They didn't so's the rail-road did. That's what you call power.

~

  Fire Hose Company Number 1 had a meeting at Thomas' lumber office. Wrote some by-laws and a constitution. Having a ball February 22. Fire-men do know how to throw a shin-dig. Oughta be fun.

February 2, 1882
  Some people don't know what's good for ém. Young Porter refused to get vaccinated even with the Mayor's order. So's 3 or 4 fellers de-coyed him into the street and dragged him into Dr. Brown's office. They laid him on the floor and sat on him while the doctor shot him with a needle of vaccine. Ain't telling no-body I lied about getting mine. Seems a right angry bunch on the matter.

February 3, 1882
  Still ain't no-one working on the water-works. Pipe dreams most likely. Mean-time, folks getting water from a wagon what drives through town selling it.

~

  Presbyterian Ladies Society gonna have a Valentine's Day festival to raise money for pews in the church. Church about to get carpet and lamps for the pulpit. It shaping up nicely.

~

  That Gold Nugget Placer Mining Company of Salida wrote what they calls a annual report. Got $500,000 and 50,000 share. Roller, C.T. Barton, and Twitchell directors. That's a bunch of money, and not one of them dudes ever bothers to buy a round.

February 4, 1882
  Trusses up for the Opera House roof.

~

Got twice the families in town what were here 6 months ago. Big ole city Salida getting.

~

Little Winnie Webb down with the pneumonia. Sad seeing a girl so sick.

~

Max Dickman building a addition to his lumber office.

~

Miss Kitty Ayers thinking of opening a select school as the one for all folks getting over-crowded.

February 5, 1882
Pink eye struck the live-stock around here. Most horses in the valley laid up with swelled legs, red eyes, and bad cold. Sure hope that ain't catching for peoples.

~

Rumor got it the Denver short line gonna start building on this end soon. If Salida rumors was gold I'd be as flat broke as I be today.

~

Uncle Dave's Saloon got a big ole hole in one of the larger window panes. Major Binckley put his cane through it, revenge for some-thing or the other.

~

Business feller dickering with Governor Hunt for the lots on the corner of E Street and First. Wanna build ém a two-story brick and stone place.

February 6, 1882
Levi Graham and Ben Nichols, 2 colored fellers over at the Junction House, had a little round-up early Sunday morning. Graham gave Nichols a tongue-lashing, calling him some fighting names right in front of folks. Vile and ugly names they be. Graham got took before Justice Bowne and plead guilty to swearing but says he ain't done no fighting. Theys had a trial and Graham got fined $10. Nichols got his-self arrested for throwing dishes and pounding on Graham. Got him $5 fine.

February 7, 1882
This town getting down-right silly with ordinances. It now against the law to break out of jail or to help another break out. Ain't that some-thing? What kinda of fool don't know it ain't law-ful to do such?

~

Town board passed a ordinance what says folks can't smoke opium. $50-$100 fine it be. That there gonna piss off the china-men. But mainly it gonna cause a storm from the whores what like to smoke. Up-setting a yellow man be one thing. Up-setting a woman, even a whore, be another.

I ain't one to lasso that level of up-set. We have whores rioting in the streets soon for sure.

February 9, 1882
Those what buy property getting rich. In September, Sweet's Block, set across the street from *The Mountain Mail*, coulda been got for $500. Worth a bunch more to-day. Mr. Williams bought a lot near the Opera House for $225 and got offered $450 only 3 days later. When the new tender-feet gets here come spring prices be higher for sure.

~

Got a new saloon. Harris opened on First Street and G with free lunch.

~

I ain't heard exactly what were said, but a young lady in town filed a law-suit against a man for slander. Pissing off women don't bring no-thing but misery. Marrying one do about the same. I learnt that the hard way when I had me a full-time, live-in woman. She were a Ute squaw what couldn't cook for shit, but she kicked harder than my mule, I guaran-damn-tee you. Still gots a few bruises what ain't never gonna heal.

~

Already the round-house needs to get bigger. Most days they got 12-15 engines waiting to get in.

~

Town board gave the thumbs up for $17,500 to build a water-works. Contract gone to Russell and Alexander. Gonna sell bonds to pay for it.

February 11, 1882
Went to the opera last night and seen a fine show. It were held in the church and every seat were sat on. Had a good number standing, them what showed up late. Serves ém right for not having manners enough to get in on time.

Had a bunch of entertain-ment. Some good. Some not. Had a quartette of men singing which weren't bad even if'n it be men. The Peaked Sisters had some songs and choruses that was pleasing. They done best on the Methodist songs. French says so any-way but don't no-body give a damn what French says.

Dr. Gibbons reading were the best part of the night most folks says. Most folks also says the solo by Mr. Case be horrid. Wouldn't of sur-rised me to see dead animals in the street when it were done. There weren't none, but damn it were pain-ful to hear the man screech.

February 13, 1882
G.S. Huggins, what got a second-hand store, got broke in to Tuesday night by a couple of damn idiots.

These fools teared off 2 or 3 boards from the rear of Huggins building. They got in-side and helped them-selves to cigars, pencils, notions, re-volvers and guns, few hundred dollars worth. Who the hell steals pencils? Any-ways, these boys musta been drunk cause theys busted out a front window when leaving. The noise woke Marshal Stingley, who was sleeping in his room up--stairs, the next building over. Stingley rushed down and caught one feller. Not long later, he caught up to the other and got back most of the stole goods. All except for a .45 Colt re-volver and 2 Sharpe's rifles. Sounds like they be another feller what didn't get caught.

John Welch and Charles T. Burgess the damn idiots what did the robbing. Got took before Judge Garrison and got $750 bonds each. Stole pencils. I swear I hope that sort of stupid ain't catching like the small-pox.

February 14, 1882
Opera House got a tin roof going up. Won't be long be-fore it opens. Be nice to have a place for shows and such what ain't in a church.

~

Got a new daily news-paper what be a month old. Lord a 'mighty that seem like a lot of work. Can't figure we gots us so much news in a town so small but if I knowed such I'd be writing for a living and not carrying folks things and sweeping floors.

~

West's block going up. Got framing done.

February 16, 1882
Seem like most the new houses what go up got 2 stories. Ain't never lived in a place so high and mighty. Got stuck in a tall tree once, and that weren't fun. I figure a house so tall be a bit similar.

~

Miss Kitty Ayers select school to open Monday in Hunt's building.

~

From what I heard from those passing through, Salida got a heap less colored folk than any town its size the State. Be fine by me if them darkies keep to other places. What with the china-men we got all the color we need here-abouts.

February 19, 1882
Yet another feller in town trying to buy a lot for a hotel. Ain't gonna be nothing but hotels, saloons, and 2-story houses soon. Long's theys room for my tent and mule I shouldn't complain. But I will.

~

Fisher's building near about done on the corner of E Street and First. Gonna be 24 feet by 50.

~

That new place, Western Hotel, got a free hack running to and from all trains. Enterprising they be. Smart too. Folks ain't gonna walk when they can climb in a carriage. Wonder where fellers get smarts like that? Me, I sleep in a tent with a farting mule. I ain't saying that be dumb, but it sure as hell ain't smart like these men.

~

Fellers busy grading this side of the track for side-walks. Ain't gonna be nothing to this town what look like country be-fore long. We citified now for sure. Ain't gonna be room for working fellers like me what don't have a tie and a cane.

Cheap Charley's Clothing House, Maysville, Colorado, 1882
Donna Nevens Collection, Salida Regional Library, Salida, Colorado

February 21, 1882

Salida got ém a small place, between Shope's Saloon and Jack McCall's Saloon, for a store-room for the fire department needs.

~

Had us some wizard tricks on stage at the church. Signore Martel done the tricks. His wife, Signora Martel, done the telling as the Mr. be a deaf mute. Grand magic it were! Had some startling wonders, like the mystery of the magical waters, Satan in a faro room, and jokes and music. Lordy, what a fun time it be. Never thought I'd laugh so much nor have a good time in-side a church. But I did!

To-morrow gonna have a big ole ball for the fire-men at Dickman's Opera House. $1.50 a ticket theys charging. I could drink all night for that but a good party it sure to be. Guess'n tough choices be part of life, but I'm hoping theys have some free liquor in-side.

February 23, 1882
Seems that coal problem got solved. Over at Roller & Twitchell's office be a big ole sample of what what came from a new coal bank found 5 miles from Salida. Some out-of-town fellers, one from Poncha Springs and one from over to Wellsville, found the strike and says it a bonanza for a fact. Means we ain't gotta keep hunting for fire-wood year-round and that a good thing. Going after fire-wood ain't no-thing but a circle of time what keep me from the saloons.

~

Streets sure dusty. Some snow or rain needed to tap it down. Too damn cold to jump in the river for washing.

~

Dr. Brown's left jaw laid up for repair. Wonder who he mouthed off to?

February 24, 1882
J.A. Waddell leased the New York House for 6 months. Yet another owner for that place. Con-found if it ain't had a bunch of folks try to make it work.

~

Folks in town seen a big ole shooting star just before 9 at night. Pretty it were. Ain't life interesting?

~

The Fire Company ball were one of the finest ever in this town. Had 9 Virginia reels going at one time on the floor. They made a mess of money too. $75 cash.

~

Damn if we ain't got a bunch of pigs running loose in town. Some-one don't get to penning ém up, Sam gonna be eating fresh bacon soon. That's a fact.

February 25, 1882
Amos Slater opened a black-smithing and wagon-making business. I always had to admire man what can work with iron and such. That there be a skill. Not like them dandy bankers and law-yers what make money moving this here pile of papers over there and that there mess of papers over here.

~

Ain't seen butter in this town in way too long. Biscuits too damn dry with-out a bit to slab on, and what grease I got ain't gonna last much longer.

~

Miss Kitty Ayers school opened with 30 students. All paying to be there. Money sure be good for some families.

February 25, 1882
That news-paper feller wrote a re-minder the town be name Sa-Lee-dah and that the proper way to say it. Damn if I hear any-one what says it that way. Sounds like a dude word if'n they ask me, which they didn't. I knowed it be proper Mexican, but Sa-Lie-Dah is what all the fellers what I know says and that just fine by me.

~

Governor Hunt bringing a bunch of trees to town but asking for promises they be cared for proper. He sent trees over to
Alamosa, and they all died cuz ain't no-one give 'em water or some such. Sounds like some-thing people down there would do. Ain't no sense amongst ém.

~

New business feller in town name Hively. Looking for a place to build a hard-ware store.

~

Benjamin F. Rock married Miss Fannie G. Bradford at his office. Weren't no-body invited.

February 26, 1882
Sam Sandusky left town. Heading to Garfield for to manage a store the Craig brothers got there. Shame. He a right kind young feller.

~

Boys of all sizes spending the warmer days playing marbles in the streets. Sure hope no pigs run ém down.

~

J.P. and George Smith shut down their dry goods and clothing partner-ship. J.P. gonna keep the dry goods business above the Bank of Salida. George, he taking the clothing store to the rear of Hartzell's bank building. Sad it be when family can't get along, but that's what money do to folks. Good thing I ain't got neither. No such worries be in my life and that just fine by me.

~

Gessert brothers opened up a restaurant and bakery on F Street, a bit down from and Corbin's place.

~

Soon we have 4 meat markets in town. That should drive the prices down to where a working man can buy some. I swear I'm tired of grease drippings and biscuits, but ain't many wagons to unload during winter. My skinny ass getting skinny-er by the day.

~

Got us a foot-race set for March 15. Wonder who the big boss gonna be?

BLACKSMITH SHOP.

AMOS SLATER,

Proprietor.

All work in the line of

BLACKSMITHING

AND

WAGON MAKING

promptly attended to.

Special attention given to horse-shoeing.

Advertisement from The Mountain Mail, 1882

CHAPTER THREE
March 1882

March 5, 1882
Harris closed his saloon. How the hell can a man not make money selling liquor in a town full of rail-road workers and drunks?

~

Edward Corbin a go-getter. He setting up a pork packing company. Wonder how a feller gets a pig to agree to such?

~

I seen a young man pull a razor on another feller last night. Weren't no cutting, just a bunch of words. Police-man Moll took the razor away, and that were that.

~

The post office moved to a new office on F Street, one door down from *The Mountain Mail*.

March 6, 1882
Baxter Stingley back in town after a trip to Gunnison. He say he were treated mighty fine by them folk. Ain't never heard much about that town other than people be kind.

~

After a bunch of fires, folks asking for a ordinance what says folks can't leave lanterns burning when they not home. Shame folks need laws to stop ém from being idiots, but such the world we have these days.

~

Got a new saloon opening Saturday! Called the Driftwood and gonna be over on Second Street. Don't know that fellers gonna walk so far to get drunk, but I might give it a go. Beggars got cheap prices, I find.

March 7, 1882
I see more and more businesses move down to F Street, near the river, and away from First and G Street. Fellers finally figuring out the closer they be to the rail-road the more money they gets. I ain't never owned no store, but I seen that fact right away. And I the one eating biscuits and grease. Life ain't got no fair-ness to it. None at all.

~

Salida Mining and Milling had a bunch of machines come in by train. Best they figure out wheres they want to put the mill. Ain't that the sort of thing you think on before spending money on fancy things? I swear money-men ain't got sense enough to not piss in their own kitchen.

March 10, 1882
Van Camp, feller what a general pain for all, got put in the calaboose

after whooping on his woman, Ella. She says they need to not be together no more. Van Camp got all girlie hurt, went to drinking hard, came home, and beat poor Ella. Some boys ain't got no more starch than a wet biscuit. Now, if she selling some on the side that one thing, but beating a woman what can't stand your face no more just be shame-ful. Sound like a man what wears women's under-wear if'n they ask me. Which they didn't.

~

Them rail-road boys know how to throw a party.
Conductors masked ball had the best music ever in Salida. 70 people had a supper over to Clarendon's restaurant. Professor Charles McKinney of Salida and Professor Ozmon of Maysville made the music. Lord, did they have some fancy costumes. Some pretty some flat out ugly ones. Folks spent a heap of time getting fancied up.
The ladies was a fine looking bunch.
Mrs. O'Brien and Mrs. Williams went as the Sisters of Charity. Miss Mary Ruefly were Morning. Mrs. Bender were Night. Miss Rosa Reed was a Lady Clown. Mollie Parsons dressed as a
Flower Girl, and Mrs. Wells was what they call a Equestrienne, which I learnt be a fancy word for horse rider. Why the hell they couldn't call it such beyond me. Mrs. Charles Mullen were a Indian Princess. Mrs. Howell be a Persian Girl. Mrs. F.P. Brown made her-self up as the Daughter of the Nile. Ada Rush were fancy as the Milky Way. Mrs. Mix wore a fancy dress. Guess'n she ain't much for costuming. Miss Bastable were a Indian Squaw. Miss Harper dressed as a Popcorn Girl, whatever the hell that is. Miss Minnie Fry were a news-paper boy, tho how a girl can be a boy confused me a tad. Mrs. Fry went as *The Mountain Mail,* and that just made me want to drink cuz it confused me so bad. Miss Aida Ayers was a Gypsy and Mrs. Hunn was the Aurora Borealis, which I got tolt be a bunch of stars so far away it can't be seen, so I ain't sure how she knowed what it look like. And Ada Rush were the Queen of the Skating Rink.
Fellers dressed up too.
I went as a miner. Didn't take much time to put that to-gether, tho I did have to wade in the river to get the dirt off my neck and privates, and brother, you ain't never seen a fast-er wash job. That water have to warm up a lot to just be cold.
R. Hallock dressed as a English Hunter. T.J. Laughlin went as Mephistopholes. J.E. Marron were a Clown. W. Scott were a Dutch Comedian, but I ain't sure how that different from any other comedian. Max Dickman were a Wise Man From the East. Mr. Zeigler were Duke Alexis, and J.M. Turner were the Prince of Wales. I'm thinking them fellers seeing their-self as more than they be, but that just my thinking. Charles Mullen went as Oscar Wilde, who some-one says be a writer. Charles Crater were Topsy. O. Lampugh were Lady Domino, which confused me as much as a woman news-paper boy. Dan Wooten dressed

as a China-Man and that one were down-right funny—tho, if he stumbled in-to the wrong saloon after, he got his-self a beating for sure. T.B. Sullivan dressed up as Germany. Doc Norton fancied up as King Henry VIII. S.G. Adams had what he call a Fancy Costume, but damn if I know what it be. L.L. Downing were Louis IX. My favorite of the night were Charles Richardson and George McClean what went as Siamese Twins. Funny as hell that were, especially when they got to drinking. George Crater were a Zulu Chief. James Bathurst were also a China-man. Sam Wooley dressed out as a Negro Comedian. W. H. Dixon had a different take on that and came as Old Darkey. J.H. Paddock were a Big Clown. Joe Meyers dressed as a Soldier, but I figure he ain't got no more imagin-ation than me and just put on his old uniform. Same with Frank Roberts who came as a Sailor Boy. Oscar Bookholtz were a Song and Dance Darkey.

A fun night it were indeed.

~

Crispell and Hakins come to town to build mills for that new company.

~

Blake headed to Fremont county after selling his stock of dry goods and clothes to Rockafellow. Damn if we ain't got some turn-over happening. He were a good feller in this town.

March 11, 1882
Man what seemed un-sound of mind came into *The Mountain Mail* office and says he got roughed up. He seemed more scared than hurt, but he weren't right in the head, that's for damn sure.

~

Fellers name Mellen and Brumfield got ém a photo-graph gallery in a tent on F Street below Gessert's bakery. Seems they fine artists from folks what know such things. Only in town a few days. Figure I take a stroll and see what fine art photo-graphs look like. Don't know I ever seen such.

~

That man Waddell, what took over managing the New York House, says it getting re-modeled with every-thing new and clean and gonna be one of the best around. That ain't but the third or fourth time I heard such, and ain't seen it happen yet.

~

Seems the question of where to put the mill been answered. Governor Hunt gave 5 acres on the upper end of the Milk Ranch, the one by George Williams Ranch. Theys got the machines there already. Lord, it a shame I ain't got no rich friends what give me land for free. But it ain't free. Any fool knows that no matter what the paper-work says. Money changed hands some ways.

March 12, 1882

Feller name P.T Pendleton got brought back to Salida for stealing a over-coat from Mr. Snyder over at Hawkins Hotel. They took him to Justice Garrison, and brother did they have the dead -wood on the man. Damn fool had the coat on him when he got caught. Got his-self fined $50 plus $125 in expenses. He ain't had such funds, and got took to Buena Vista where he gonna spend time in the county calaboose.

Had a nice little wedding in town. Willis P. Brown married Miss Annie E. Meyers. The Bales, French's, Tallman's were there plus Miss Kitty Ayers and her guest.

National Meat Market, Granite, Colorado, 1880
Patricia Bradbury Holton Collection, Salida Regional Library, Salida,

March 13, 1882

Lord a mighty, but it were a hot time at the cat-house and not in a fun way.

About half-past 3 in the morning, every-one heard re-volvers shooting and train whistles blowing. A fire it were and a big one. At the whore-house to boot.

Folks come running in-to the streets and seen Lizzie Langdon's house, the one on G Street next to the alley between First and Second, and brother it were burning like it were the last fire on earth. Langdon be the madam folks call White Dog Liz on account of she always gots a little white dog in her arms, and it always be spot-less. That dog a damn site cleaner than most fellers in town. There weren't no way to save the place it were so full of flames.

Folks in-side barely got out with what clothes they could grab.

Seems the fire started some sort of way in the kitchen. Probably a lantern or a flue what weren't put in proper.

House were full of working girls and some paying customers. One of them fellers woke up smelling smoke. He took to looking around and seen the blaze. He threw on his pants but seems $200 fell out of his pocket and that were burned up. Feller cut his foot some-thing fierce kicking out a window. Seems the fool ain't thought to shove at least one boot on his bare feets.

Ms. Langdon's house cost $1800 to build and had it a $100 piano inside. I ain't never spent no time there, but I went in once before they throwed me out on account of me smelling awful and not having cash money. Pretty it were, tho. Seems Langdon had some insurance, about $500, but it going to a feller name Otis White, what had a loan on the property.

Lucky there weren't no wind and we still got us snow on roof-tops. If not, the town be gone up in flames for sure the fire were so big.

That good news ain't helping the feller with the cut foot who out $200. I laughed seeing him hop around bare-chested with his bloody foot. All he could scream about was his money. I'm guessing he ain't got no woman to explain things to.

March 14, 1882

Seen Howell and McClean get into it. Had a knock-down, drag-out. McCLean got away with Howell in the first round, and looked in good shape. Howell got knocked down before he knowed what happened.

~

Marshal Stingley checking for trash in alleys and back yards, and it about time. A mess it were here. I ain't living in town, but I sure don't like the look and smell of folks tossing stuff out their door. Good for the Marshal.

~

We gots more thieving going on than any proper place should have. Ain't gonna do much for the boys what stealing if'n
    they get caught. That I guarandamntee you.

~

Seems we got a foot race gonna happen soon. Boys I know saving their change for betting.

~

With all the new folks moving in town wonder why don't some-one build a bunch of small places to rent? I ain't one for business, but seems to be there be proper money to be made. Sue and me down-right happy in our tent, even if she do be a farting engine.

March 15, 1882

I knowed some mean fellers in my day, but a man what steal from a child is a special kind of mean. One what ought to get up close and personal with a rope if'n they ask me, which they didn't.

Little Willie Mix, 3-year-old what broke his leg a few weeks ago, got all his nickels stoled. Cock-sucker what took the money stoled the damn bank, too. Little boy saved his-self 6 whole dollars which ain't no little amount. Mr. Mix says he know damn well who the thief be, and theys gonna get arrested soon. He put up a reward of $25 if'n the thief get put in jail.

~

Them news-paper fellers, Moore and Olney, dis-solved their partnership. Olney retiring, so Moore gonna run the paper business by his lone-some.

~

Folks talking theys too many vagrants and dead-beats in this town. Me, I keep busy when people watching, on account a I ain't want to be in that group. Folks get power-ful angry thinking loafers be around. I might not have a full-time paying job, but I buys my own drinks and meals. Less'n a feller be blind drunk and offers up a round. My momma ain't raised no fool.

March 16, 1882

Fellers what know about such things says to buy property now as it going up big-time in the next 60 days, and then it be pricey for good. Land my tent on ain't cost no-thing, and it good enough for me and Sue.

~

I heard the Lotus Club having a phantom party at Dickman's Opera House soon. Invites coming, but don't think I be on the list.

~

Some smart aleck cut Sing Lee's laundry line. That ain't right. I ain't fond of them yellow fellers, but whacking away a man's business is plain ole hate-ful. Sing, he says he "must look little out maybe so I catch him next time." That kind of talk ain't good for no-thing. This town gonna blow up if'n a yellow man starts to beating on a white feller.

March 17, 1882

J.F. Welsh, laborer at the stone quarry below town, were in Salida Monday night and got on a tear. He threw big words at police-man Modie. Modie later arrested the feller for making his-self too familiar with some young ladies on the street. Welsh, fool he be, fought Modie and kicked up a deuce of a rumpus. Got his-self fined for drunk and disorderly when the judge heard about it.

March 18, 1882

Stranger name Brooks were here a short while, and brother did he cause some commotion. A young feller, 30-year-old from Ireland, stout and hardy and smooth-faced. He engaged the Opera House for his company, the National Opera Combination. Booked it for both Friday and Saturday night.

When all were said and done, Brooks stood off the printer for the bill, Dickman for the hall rental, and Hawkins for the hotel charges.

Friday came and went, but no show were held. Saturday there were a show, and brother what a show it were! If'n you missed the show you missed out for sure. There only be 7 ladies, a few men, and a bunch of noisy young men and boys watching. I were one of the fools what paid to see it. When the curtain come up weren't nothing but Brooks, a couple of darkies from Hawkins Hotel, 2 or 3 boot-blacks, and a bunch of supes.

All the ladies left in the first 2 minutes cuz the show were what they says be disgusting. Only me and them young fellers stayed. And I stay only cuz it were the most down-right silly thing

I ever seed. Brooks were so drunk he fell off the stage. The boys gave Brooks a standing ovation for that act.

Next day, Brooks jaw-boned all for what he owed. Went over to Ryan's livery and rented a team to take his show to Poncha. When he got back, the team were jaded, and the buggy damn near demolished. Ryan whacked Brooks over the head with a club and swore out a warrant for vagrancy and swindling. Brooks got more free lodging that night in the calaboose.

Justice Garrison heard from all what Brooks owed and says it worth $100 cash money, but gave Brooks 2 hours to ske-daddle from town, and that what Brooks done. He gone now! Didn't leave so much as a lock of hair. Lots of folks got un-used tickets to his show. Feller got big balls, I declare. Says those what head over to Poncha to-night get in the show for free.

March 19, 1882

With all the dang building, hammering day and night still, ain't a carpenter in miles what ain't working if'n he wants.

~

Rail-road putting more side tracks on this side of the river.

~

Theys asked, but Mr. Bateman don't want to be a town trustee no more. Says he too busy. Smart feller what don't wade deep in-to politics. Wish more fellers was so bright.

~

Folks saying Salida need to buy the town ditch what now owned by Kelsey, Haskell and Blake. Sounds right. We need control over what happens here.

March 22, 1882
Miss Kitty Ayers shut down her school as she ain't a school marm no more. Got her-self married.

~

Got another new hotel, The Western, owned by George W. Cline.

~

The Park block opened, but it sure need a bunch of improving.

~

Food looking up. They be radishes, onions, and lettuce on the market now that spring-time come.

March 23, 1882
The Devine building in place near the east end of F Street bridge. It 20 by 60 feet, 2 stories, and got a restaurant.

~

Yet more grocery fellers in town. Bissell and Bates opened 2 doors down from *The Mountain Mail* office.

~

The neighbor-hood betwixt F Street and Second shaping up. Lots of new buildings. Ain't no little town no more.

March 24, 1882
Up F Street, in the old post office stand, in the rear of Blake's dry good store, be a place opened by new fellers, Hively and Young. Theys gonna sell hard-ware, tin-ware, stoves, cutlery, lamps, chandeliers, and all that fancy kind of crap. La-te-dah, I says. They already doing tin roofing and sheet iron work. These 2 young fellers some busy bees. Good crafts-men for sure even if'n they selling fancy woman-type things.

~

Feller name Frank Roberts, what some called 'Skinny" skipped out 2 weeks ago. He did type-setting at the news-paper, but seems he did some lifting too. A coat and a pair of boots went missing from *The Mountain Mail,* plus things from his boarding house and some stores in town. Roberts were 30 or 35 in age, 5 feet 6 or 7 inches tall, and one of those fellers what can't keep his tongue still under any consideration. Easy enough to notice as'n he can't say 3 words with-out profanity. I suffer the same ailment, but I ain't no thief.

March 26, 1882
Even with them ordinances, we still gots lots of stock roaming town. Wish the law were as tolerant with us drunks being disorderly. Life sure ain't fair.

~

Beebe and Mix teamed up to make bricks. Burning 100,000 bricks soon's they build the kiln.

News-paper pushing hard for folks to plant thousands of trees in town. Would go a long way to keeping the dust down. Wouldn't mind shade neither come summer.

Elections coming again. Got 2 parties: Citizens and People's. On the Citizens ticket be O.V. Wilson for mayor, C.F. Gatliff clerk/recorder, M.M. French, L.W. Craig, J.A. Israel, and A.W. Jones trustee. On the People's ticket be E.H. Webb mayor, F.D. Howell clerk/recorder, J.A. Israel, A.W. Jones, R. Devereaux, and W.E. Robertson trustee.

March 27, 1882

Van Every moving his house from Bale's Ranch to Second Street opposite Jesse Brown's Saloon. Ain't gonna be nothing left in Cleora soon.

Church folks taking over town. A Catholic one heading to town.

Town sure look better now the marshal's crews raked all the trash out the streets.

Lordy, we getting fancy. Clark and Stewart put a big ole mirror in their place. It 6 feet by 8 feet and hanging behind the bar. French plate, heavy fame. It's a beauty, but I ain't gonna look in it much as what look back don't show nothing but wrinkles and gray.

Snow melting fast. River be up high soon.

March 30, 1882

Hills betwixt the rail-road track and the mountains, near the depot, thick as flies with small houses. Can't walk 10 feet with-out bumping in-to a shack.

I swear I shoulda learnt the grocery business. Webb, what part of Webb and Corbin Grocery, same feller running for mayor, bought 4 lots from Roller and Twitchel on the corner of Fifth Street and F. Putting a water line in it and planning a grand home. Even gonna have the plans on exhibit at his store in April. Ain't that uppity?

CHAPTER FOUR
April, 1882

April 1, 1882
A.B. Chapline meeting April 5 at Hunt's building for talk on bringing a Knights of Pythias lodge to Salida.

~

Arkansas Valley Mining and Milling Company incorporated with Thomas Cobb, C.B. Underhill, A.M. Alger, Charles E. Tucker, A. Lindsay, L. Whitmer, and B. Applegate directors. These fellers got 160 acres 1 mile west and 4 miles above town on the river.

~

About midnight Thursday, folks what live down-town got woke straight up with gun-fire. W.L. Whann, Ed. Streepy, R. Devereaux (saloon feller running for trustee), and Dick Devereaux got arrested. No one seen Streepy shooting, and the law turned him loose right away. Whann paid up his fines, $10 cash, but the Devereaux's says they ain't paying shit and taking it to court.

April 2, 1882
The Opera House looking mighty fine now theys put a new coat of paint on. Up-town it be.

~

Beebe and Mix finished their kiln, and loading it fast as possible but says they can't keep good workers. Brick-making hard work for sure. Harder than I wants to do.

~

I swear I seen it all now. Sure enough. Ole Corbin took to panning gold right from the dirt on F Street. Seen it with my own eyes. Says he gonna stake the town and run all the dirt through the mill. Now ain't that some-thing? Not only ain't I seen gold in the river where I fishing, I ain't even seen it right under my damn feet. Life sure ain't fair.

April 3, 1882
Charlie Hawkins and C.T. Lahr says they found another stone quarry a mile above town by Beebe and Mix's brick-yard. Says they a mountain of it to be had.

~

New saw-bones in town, name Dr. Gordon. Quartering in a place above Roller and Twitchell's furniture store. He been out west most of his life, and says he well-suited to treating illness what found in the wilderness.

~

A new addition been laid out on the south-east edge of town. This one done by Blake, Hodgman, and Westerfield. Gonna plat out streets running square with the world, not following the rail-road like the first. They says they to have 2 or 3 broad avenues and 4 rows of trees between them. They plans to make it the finest in town.

~

Election done. Wilson beat out Webb for mayor 198-158. Howell lost to Gatliff for clerk/recorder 195-118. Heard lots of false stories about Webb during the contest, but Webb kept quiet, thinking his reputation would take care of the lies. It ain't. Good men all were elected, tho.

April 5, 1882

The Opera House and the whole Wheeler block got new side-walks. Lordy, we getting fancy in this town. Soon ain't gonna be a muddy boot to be seen.

~

Got the first rain of the season Tuesday. About damn time. Dust were caking on top of the dust.

~

F Street looking to be the place for business. Blake thinking of turning his store so's it facing F Street, right next to Hively, Young and Company. If he do, he gonna add a two-story brick building where there now be wood frame.

~

Seen the city made budget for $2500 for marshal and police services, $1000 for streets, $1500 for water, $1000 for attorney, $1000 for fire department, $500 for the city park, and $500 for town clerk.

April 6, 1882

Another new ordinance calls for 6 lamps on the F Street bridge so's folks don't go falling over the side. Marshal in charge of lighting ém at dark and putting ém out at dawn. $50-$100 fine for damaging or breaking.

~

New ordinance calls for $10-$100 for assault and battery. Good God almighty, we need laws now to tell folks you can't go to beating on a man for no good cause? What next? Gonna tell folks theys ought not to crap their pants? Stupid times these be.

~

Mrs. Bender joking that if'n a woman wants to get married all she gots to do is come work in her kitchen. Poor lady can't keep help. Of course, when theys ain't but a hand-ful of single women, not counting whores and such, ain't no surprise they get snatched up faster than free candy.

April 9, 1882

Folks digging new ditches on lots of streets in town. Trying to settle the damn dust, and that okay by me. If'n it stay this dusty I gonna have to start bathing damn near every week.

~

New show in town! Professor Allen and his colored gentle-men minstrels be here. Count me in.

~

Bateman following the others and putting a new front on his store to face F Street along with Hively and Young. F Street the official main street it seems. First and Second less import-ant every day.

~

Marshal Stingley got his jail crews digging holes around town to plant trees, particularly around Alpine Park. He sure seem intent on sprucing up Salida.

~

Salida Land Company jumping in on the trees. Planting 500-600 around their un-sold lots. Ain't gonna be much of the desert left before long. Won't hear me complaining when shade be needed come summer.

April 11, 1882

Beebe and Mix got 30,000 bricks in the kiln. Theys a busy couple of fellers.

~

F.S. and W.J. Hartzell bought the Bank of Salida from F.W. DeWalt. DeWalt going to Leadville to run his bank there. The Hartzell's already own Custer County Bank in Silver Cliff. Seems they spreading it thin to me, but what I know of banking wouldn't fill a half-filled bucket.

~

Dr. Gordon moving already. New office to be in the room vacated by Walker the barber.

~

Max Dickman got a new safe in his lumber office. Only took him and his clerks a half day to open it. The boys was laughing hard at that one but Dickmans says A.T. Ryan and Judge Bowne was the ones what couldn't get the dang thing open. Ain't heard Ryan and the judge's take on the matter.

~

Ran in to Mrs. Reed who says she be obliged if the parties what took 3 or 4 silk hand-kerchiefs from her clothes line would bring them back. Can't imagine it hard to see such things in use around town.

~

Salida Land Company agents, Roller and Twitchell, ordered a car-load of broad leaf cotton-wood trees for town. Says they ordering more if'n they can find some.

~

Jesse Stingley, the Marshal's brother, married Miss Nettie M. Cameron at the home of her father, Thomas Cameron. The Naylor's was there, the Coffey's, the Reeds with their daughter, Miss Cameron's parents and brother and sister, Baxter Stingley, of course, and Ernest Christison. That last one odd, as'n he one of the fellers Baxter Stingley help run out of the valley back in the Lake County War days. Time heals all they says.

April 13, 1882

Some-one stoled a buffalo robe, 3 blankets, and a comforter from the rear of the *Mail* office. Them fellers gets more things stoled than any-one I know.

April 14, 1882

Salida soon be stepping in high cotton. The great violinist, Ede Remenyi, and his troupe, will perform at Dickman's Opera House on the 25th. He a feller from across the ocean in a place they call Hungary. I got tolt it ain't like when you ain't ate in days but different. *New York Post* news-paper says he the best violinist ever to play in this country. *New York Herald* says he a master of the instrument. 75 cents it cost to hear the feller. Ain't never heard no violin player, just fiddle scratchers. Gonna have to get me a job so's I can go hear the difference.

~

We ain't all that high-class just yet. Feller name Pierce got his-self arrested for licking a woman. I shit you not. And she weren't even a whore. Judge Bowne fined him $10 cash money, but as'n Pierce ain't got no funds he went to work for the city.

~

By God, some men like to flap their jaws like a proper lady's lap dog. Colonel Tom Fielding and Major Dave Shope been carrying on 2 days about what a prize fight they gonna have. The way it going, all's gonna happen is the Colonel gonna put his tongue out of joint and the Major gonna get his chin wiped off. Such yipping there be with no-thing to show.

April 16, 1882

Sweet baby Jesus, but we got snow again. Ain't it ever gonna stop? I'm hoping this one be the last. My ole bones need some sun.

~

Painter, what does art, not buildings, in town by name of Jack Williams. Has him a exhibit at Dickman's. Black and whites and color pictures made of oil. I ain't never seen such, and gonna head over for sure. Don't know I ever see no-thing what you'd call art.

~

Got a tooth doc moving to town name Dr. W.K. Eggleston. He from back east in Philadelphia. Gonna office at the Mix House.

Yet again, the Junction House changed hands. Feller name Maguire, from Pueblo, the new new owner. That place a regular carousel.

Seen a big load of trees come in by train for the Salida Land Company. Feller in charged refused ém, cuz they all too small.

April 17, 1882
Night watch-man over to the depot grabbed a man what was getting ready to steal a ride to Pueblo. He seen the car seal were broke, and took the feller over to the Marshal. The ride thief says a brake-man let him in and charged him $2 for the ride. Sounds about right, but the man still be arrested.

That Remenyi feller, one what plays violin, headed this way after big ole shows in Denver and Colorado Springs. Folks out that way says it the show to see.

There a blanket thief in town. Feller must be frightful cold cuz he struck again. Took blankets and bedding from a tent on Second Street, opposite the black-smith shop.

Salida Banks' safe a safe one for sure. Make no mistake. The bank set the time lock by accident, and it were shut tight all day Monday. They couldn't get no money until after banking hours. The boys sure had a lot of fun over this.

April 18, 1882
Joshua Allen hired a young man to advertise his show and sell tickets. The feller were so promiscuous and full of fire, not letting people pass and such that Allen fired the man and then spent half of Saturday night looking for the feller to give him a beating.

Speaking of beatings, Assistant Marshal Modie got beat on when he were making rounds on Second Street near the Driftwood. Modie a tough one, tho. After the fight, he arrested Charles Rollinton and tossed him in jail. $35 fine. Loose woman name Anna Layton or Lawrence, I ain't sure which, got arrested for helping out, but judge turned her loose.

Another new ordinance says it il-legal to have a concealed weapon. $100 fine.

E. Shaul's Merchandise Sample Room, Granite, Colorado, 1880
Patricia Bradbuy Holton Collection, Salida Regional Library, Salida, Colorado

April 21, 1882

About half past 6 in the morning, fire and smoke seen coming from Mr. Frame's home, over on corner of G Street and Second. Bunch of us ran over, but it were too far gone to do any-thing but watch the burn. The Frame house also were lived in by Mr. W.E. Robertson and his wife. All 4 lost all their goods and money. $2300 worth. Only had $800 in insurance.

Van Every had a vacant building next door, and it burnt down too. 2 young fellers, W.P. Brown and David Meyers had all their traps and goods in the empty house.

The other side of the street, where Mr. Reed, Mr. Lindsay, and Mr. Bennett all got homes, plus the Driftwood Saloon be there, got saved when folks hustled over with water and wet blankets.

Ain't no one sure how the fire started. Mr. Frame woke at 6 to go open up at his job at Webb and Corbin's Grocery. His wife seen the fire a short while later and gave the alarm, but it were too late to help.

Folks stepped up to help them young fellers, ones with the traps and such, as they ain't got no insurance or no-thing.

This seals it that we need a water-works in town.

April 22, 1882

Seen Baxter Stingley and his brother Jesse with their father. He came in from Kansas. Them boys ain't seen their papa in 17 years, and that be a mighty long time. Last I see my folks I weren't but 16. Took off running and got out of town fast as I could which were a good thing. Least ways for a man what likes his hide attached to his body or don't want to see life from a rope.

~

It the week for parents. W.W. Roller's folks came from Kansas like the Stingley's. Don't know they knowed one another. Roller's papa heading to Gunnison County to look at mining property. I knowed Roller be from money. Ain't many working fellers getting rich in Salida.

~

I heard theys now 42 rail-road engineers living in Salida. A regular DandRG town this be.

~

I doing the 2-step in the streets. Got us a genuine bath-house gonna open in the old Bank of South Arkansas building. Owned by John Nugent. Not getting my jewels froze off bathing in the river fine by me, yes sir, mighty fine. Can't re-call a proper bath with hot water. I knowed I had one, but that were long ago, before coming to this Valley.

~

City doing a dance their own damn self. Finally got ém a sucker to buy the water-works bonds. Mr. Cole from Chicago paying 92 cents on the dollar.

April 23 1882
Roller and Twitchell be big business, and that's a fact. Signed up with a few large insurance companies so's they can sell such things to everyone. Well, they says they don't insure tents nor mules, but most everyone.

~

Blake contracted with W.C. Richardson to build a store-room next to the post office. Gonna be 20 feet by 40 feet, but only 1 story. Gonna be for the post office to move in so's they have more room. Salida getting so big the mail now bursting out.

~

Craig Brothers building a vault in the ground at the rear of their store. It large enough to throw all their goods in if'n theys be a fire, which theys sure to be. It 4 or 5 feet below ground with 2 feet of earth on top. Fire proof they says.

~

Mrs. Carpenter the busy bee in town. Starting to give music lessons and plans to open a millinery and dress-making shop. As'n I don't need none of them things, I ain't likely to darken her door-step, but nice to see hard working people's. And happy I be I ain't one of ém.

April 26, 1882

Well slap my be-hind and call me a new-born. My ears feel new as a store-bought coat. The largest audience I ever seen were at Dickman's Opera House, Tuesday, to see that famous violinist, Remenyi. And brother, that feller could play. Brought a damn tear to my eye, it did. I shit you not.

If'n the music in heaven be prettier I'll be surprised like a drunk finding a dollar coin in his pocket at the end of the night. It weren't no fiddle music. I ain't never heard no-thing like it. Some of it were a bit high-fluting, but still pretty to hear. Weren't no screeching nor dancing nor no-thing. Just folks sitting still letting them tunes sit in the air for them to hear. Before Remenyi played, Miss Nason and Mr. DeCelle sang. They won't never be confused with heaven music, that's for damn sure. Common-place they were. Don't I sound all uppity and society-like?

April 27, 1882

Had us a killing of sorts. About 6 in the morning, Marshal Stingley got called from bed by Edward Streepy who says J.W. Cozad were lying near death. Cozad also says a man at the dance hall had Cozad's watch.

Marshal got his-self out of bed and went to town to check things out. He found Cozad in bed in a room he rented over the

Clarendon Restaurant. Doc got called, but Cozad got worser and worser and died at 9 in the fore-noon.

Stingley found the feller what had Cozad's watch. He were too drunk to rightly say how he came to have it so's the Marshal tossed the man in jail. Sober, the feller says it were Streepy his-self what gave him the watch. Says it weren't stoled. A warrant were writ for Streepy and Deputy Sheriff Mix arrested him for thieving. He also arrested a dance hall girl name Curly.

Friends of Cozad says he got drugged and robbed of $300 cash money plus the watch. Turns out the watch belong to Marshal Stingley. It were loaned. Marshal tele-graphed Buena Vista for the coroner to come figure things out.

Cozad been working for Devereux in his saloon and were knowed to carry a big wad of money around. Free and care-less he were. Every-one knowed he got on a spree of late of late, spending here and there like it weren't no-thing. He left his job at 7 the night before and headed to his room as always. Poor feller ain't stepped out of that bed again.

Coroner ain't yet figured it all out 'cept to says he think it were poison.

April 28, 1882

Watt and Hughes closed their saloon. Says they too many in town and they ain't making no money.

~

Got lamp posts at foot of F Street bridge. Lamps to come. Regular city life we got now, and I can't says I be impressed. Noisy, crowded, and expensive. But we got plenty of saloons and whores. Some-times a feller gots to make tough choices. That's a stone-cold fact.

~

DandRG appointed a doctor at this point, Dr. F.P. Brown.

~

H.C. Chenowest painting the drop curtain for the stage at Dickman's Opera House. Pretty it be. In the center a beautiful landscape. Around it got spaces for advertising cards. The curtain ain't near done, but it certain the feller knows how to handle a paint-brush.

~

Town board says 'yes' to getting water from Haskell, Kelsey, White, and Blake. $35 each month.

~

I swear the money men keep getting richer. Webb, Corbin, and A.W. Jones bought 300 lots in town to build on and sell. They damn near own every-thing a man can see. Except my tent and I suspect theys want that too.

April 29, 1882

The good Lord likes to re-mind me why I ain't suited for a full-time, sleep-over woman. The Briggs, a family what always have un-pleasantness going, found a new way to stir the pot. They lives over on E Street and First. But they done filed for di-vorce.

Mrs. Briggs showed up the oter morning to get her piano, which she rented out to the Remenyi troupe. She found all the doors on her house locked. Sassy woman she be. Picked up a ax what lay on the porch and took to whacking her way in-side. She had the piano loaded up when Mr. Briggs showed up and says it need to go back in the house. Mrs. Briggs ain't un-loaded. She drove the wagon straight to the Opera House.

Such a rumpus them 2 kick up. And folks wonder why I'm happier than a pig in slop with my mule and tent.

~

I swear things getting peculiar around here. Went down to the depot and looked over to the tele-graph office and seen what look like a big ole pair of spectacles. George Sheehey, a rail-road engineer, put the strange thing up over the tele-graph office door. Says it called Nunn's Rail-way Telegraph or Train Order Signals. Says it new in these parts but be a better way of signaling what easier to see and under-stand. Still look like damn spectacles to me.

~

Henry and Max Dickman dis-solved their business, Dickman and Sons. Henry says he getting too old. Max gonna run things on his own going forward.

G. F. BATEMAN,

DEALER IN
Hardware and Stoves.

Jobbing in Tinware a Specialty.

Tin Roofing and Job Work of all kind.

Heavy sheet Iron Work on Short Notice.

Building Paper and Builders' Hardware.

☛ SALIDA,   -   COLO.

Advertisement from The Mountain Mail, 1882

CHAPTER FIVE
May, 1882

May 1, 1882
Finally got us a bath-house. Opened in the old South Arkansas Bank building. Lordy be, I gets a hot bath. If'n I never wash in a cold river again it be too soon. From the stink we got amongst folks in town the place gonna be a boom for sure.

~

Businesses crowding up on F Street. Every-one done figured being close to the depot good for making money. Ain't they the smart ones to learn folks rather spend money with-out walking all the way in-to town?

~

Theys building a store-house for the road master over near the depot.

~

J.H. Hughes gonna re-open the Bank Exchange Saloon. Guess he figure he gots a better way to make it what the last feller ain't had.

May 2, 1882
Got us small-pox every which way you look. Doc says to get vaccinated. Don't rightly warm up to a man poking me with a needle. Think I'll hunker down in my tent and see which way this thing blows.

~

The law actually fined some-one for some-thing other than drunk and disorderly. Edward Gaby the first one charged for that
new law against letting stock roam in town. About damn time. Folks sick of stepping in or around cow piles.

~

Israel got tired of living up-stairs, and he fitting out a house in the rear of Mulvaney's store.

~

Mr. Carpenter fixing up the place next to Alger's drug store. Gonna do watch-making and sell jewelry. This the building what used to house Charley Thomas' hardware store.

~

Salida got a new tele-graph office manager. Feller name Dan Creamer from Chillicothe, Missouri.

~

Jack Williams building opposite the West block. Gonna have him a 1-story place, 16 by 30 feet.

May 3, 1882
A new dentist, W.A. Smith, set to take in patients starting next week. Don't rightly see his place being in my path. He gonna office in

the new small place Westerfield, built behind the real estate office on the corner of F Street and First. Dr. O'Connor to be there too.

~

Speaking of Westerfield, his new addition, the one he building with Blake, coming up fast. J.A. Robertson and H.C. Pomeroy, both from Colorado Springs, bought lots. Robertson building a house there. He in town to open a transfer wagon on West's block. Pomeroy got him 2 lots and gonna run a restaurant and lunch-room.

~

The Clarendon Restaurant now in the hands of Dr. E.A. Gordon. George Hatch manager.

~

Billy Taylor of Alpine got arrested by Deputy Sheriff Nat Ray. Took him to Buena Vista. Taylor sold a mining claim what weren't his to sell. He also got caught with a Winchester rifle and other things what weren't his.

~

School district met and agreed to use the lot Governor Hunt gave for a new school building. It's a half-block stretch between Third and Fourth Street and D & E.

~

Woodring's brick making operation going well. He gots 50,000 already. Ain't got a clue where he's gonna sell ém, as folks I see still putting up wood buildings.

~

Police-man Jeff Modie back on duty, but ain't right yet from the bruises he got from that beating he took a few nights back.

May 4, 1882

Twitchell, Roller, and Hodgman all gots a bunch of fruit trees and shrubs to plant around their homes. Next, they be having white picket fences and doilies on the table. Ain't much room left for working fellers what don't use the proper fork.

~

Mrs. S.T. Lewis opening a millinery and ready-made dress shop next week in the room betwixt Wheeler's hardware and the Opera House. I re-call weren't long ago the only women's out this way were whores, and none of them worried much about pretty dresses or fancy hats. Still got plenty of sporting girls in town, but they ain't as loud in public as they once was.

~

Lotus Dancing Club having the last hop of the season, Thursday over to the Opera House. I'm thinking of visiting the bath-house be-fore. All these fancy women's in town don't seem to take kindly to a bit of odor on a man. I swear, they gonna city-fy me yet.

~

I'm thinking it near about time to light out for other parts. Another damn bunch of law-yers in town. J.R. Kennemur from Nathrop and S.W. Taylor partnered up. Opening in Judge Bowne's building, the one last used for White Brothers Meat Market. Seems to me a meat market is right proper for legal men. They sees every-one as cattle for slaughtering.

~

Beebe and Mix con-tracted with George Watson to mould and set a kiln with 100,000 bricks to be ready in a month.

May 5, 1882

I heard the new fancy folks talking how Salida would look better if th rough board buildings had a coat of white-wash. I'm thinking Salida would look better if those snooty fuckers went back east with their money and their attitudes.

~

New grocery in town, Bissell and Bates. Ain't had one of those pop up in some time.

~

Well la-te-da, ain't we upper crust now? Clark and Stewart's bar put in a water cooler. It's a dandy for sure. Ain't that some-thing? Fellers can't even dip their hat in the river no more nor pull a bucket from the well. A water cooler. I shit you not.

~

Seen a old guy from Gothic wandering town the last few days. He always drunk, which ain't no big thing, but a loafer following him all over the town. Wants to rob the old feller, I'm sure. Marshall arrested the old feller for public drunk, mainly to keep him from getting his head bashed in by the loafer. Judge fined the old man $5. Loafer were given until sun-down to leave town and leave he did.

May 7, 1882

Listening around town, folks says we needs a tailor, a foundry, a dairy, and a tele-phone exchange. City folks done took over for sure. What's wrong with a feller stitching up his own pants, milking a cow, and walking over to a neighbors when talking is needed? I swear, folks do like complicating life.

~

Them grocery fellers around town fighting big time now. Theys took to delivering groceries. What the world coming to when a person can't walk to the store and carry their own box?

~

Rail-road adding more stalls to the round-house. Gonna be a half circle when done. Theys also putting up a duplicate building north of the one what be there now. Gonna be a 40 by 80 foot machine shop.

~

I seen work crews digging grounds for that new county hospital what been promised for a while. Feller name Roberts heading up the men doing the digging. Says they be done by July. I guess it's needed, as'n I been told Salida to have 2500 people here by Christmas. It weren't but 2 years ago only a hand-ful of us called this area home. Gonna be big as Denver soon.

May 8, 1882

Yet another grocery in town. James West set up a shop on F Street and Second.

~

Seen where White Brothers putting screens around their meat market to keep all the damn flies out. Seems right smart to me.

~

Miss Jennie Wells opening a restaurant in them new rooms set up opposite Roller and Twitchell's furniture store. She a good cook for sure.

~

Big changes in the southern part of Salida over the last 30 days. Westerfield and Hodgman bought 40 acres and now got over 1000 trees, a few houses, and water going to both sides of every street. It a superior area for sure. I see where the high-flutin gonna be living soon. Them boys built proper they did. The area set to compass points, not all wonky-jawed like the town company done. Every block gots shade trees, too. On the north line is Park Avenue. It a wide street with 2 rows of trees in the center and 1 on each side. Running north and south, through the center, is Palmer Avenue what also gots 2 rows of trees down the middle. Them boys even hired men to water the trees and keep 'em healthy. I swear Salida be a money town. A damn shame to old working men like me.

May 11, 1882

Grocery stores popping up here like it were in the early days. L.A. Mandevilles got him a store now on First Street betwixt E and F.

~

Joseph Hutchinson, feller what were out here before any of us, took sick with nerve pains.

~

I heard another news-paper trying to give it a go. This one be a democratic paper. That make 6 or 7, last I counted.

~

This town ain't got many whores around of late. Theys all went over to Buena Vista on account of they got a big ole grand jury meeting there for a while. Them girls are go-getters for sure.

~

Pomeroy, new feller from Colorado Springs, bought Westerfields' real estate agency.

May 12, 1882
   Seen what I never thought I'd see in these parts. We got night lights burning now. On Front Street, right in front of Hawkins Hotel and Wilson's Grocery, theys burning lamps every night.

~

   School don't seem to be growing fast as town. Gots 72 childrens enrolled, but only 55 show up most days. The rest of 'em seems busy bothering drinking fellers like me or playing games in the street. Those what do show up got some awards. Sophy Ruefly were noted for good deportment, Harry Tallman and James Smith for full attendance.

~

   I heard them money fellers, Roller and Twitchell, sold a few hundred lots lately for homes. Denver ain't gonna have nothing on this area before long.

May 14, 1882
   Seems news-paper fellers heading to Salida like there be a gold rush. I heard rumors we gots at least 2 more coming this way—a Democratic paper and a Republican or independent.

~

   Feller in the saloon says Salida got more buildings going up than any city in the county.

~

   J.P. Smith opened up a dry goods and notions store.

~

   I seen a round-up! Bunch of dance hall girls had at it, throwing stones and such. One of 'em got arrested. They all paid their fines, made up, and went home. Man can't never find sign of what makes sense in a woman's heart.

~

   John Kelly, a common loafer and scalawag, stole shirts from a clothes-line near the river. Judge Bowne tracked him down, threw him in the calaboose, and fined the feller $10. Loafer ain't got no money, so's he working in the streets.

~

   Our days with-out sickness gone for sure. Got measles around town now. My tent seems safer every week.

May 15, 1882
   John Roberts, a young man what been laying around saloons in town a few months, scraping funds to-gether as a roust-about and pretending to be a gambler, has had 2 or 3 bad breaks. Yester-day night he went too far. Marshal Stingley and police-man Modie went to take him in. Had to call him back with gun-shots when Roberts tried to run away. Got charged with carrying a concealed weapon and resisting arrest. He pled guilty. This the second time he charged with such, so's the Judge laid it

on him and fined $50 plus court costs. Brother, that's some serious cash. Roberts ain't got such money, so's he joining the others on the road work crew.

~

Joseph Hutchinson died at 7 in the morning. He were at his home, 3 miles west of Salida. Ain't sure what caused it, but he suffered from nerve pains of the face and head a long time. Jo Hutch one of the first fellers out this way, came out 17 years ago when weren't much here but Injuns and elk and deer. Came out as agent for Bailey and Gaff to take charge of their stock interests. Feller were only 45-years-old when he died. Came to the Valley from Dearborn County, Indiana where he were orphaned.

Signed up in the war and were a lieutenant. Served with Banks on the great Red River expedition. He made and lost a couple of fortunes out here. Messed with mining some, but mainly in cattle business. Last year, he ain't done much but farming. I figure the pains slowed him down a good bit. Got his-self elected to the lower house of the Legislature in 1878, and I think served on the Colorado Territorial Legislature to boot. Lately, he were a county commissioner. Left behind a wife and a host of childrens.

Williard's Hotel, Granite, Colorado, 1880
Patricia Bradbuy Holton Collection, Salida Regional Library, Salida, Colorado

May 17, 1882

The big ole grand jury in Buena Vista indicted 17 fellers. One were Andrew Lindsay, old Scottish man knowed by all in Salida. Surprised the hell out of me and most fellers I knowed. Seems Lindsay partnered up with J. Phelan to go in-to the furniture business in Poncha Springs. Got goods from Roller and Twitchell to sell on co-mission. Took out a mortgage to secure the goods. Phelan says he ain't knowed no-thing about no mortgage and figures Lindsay signed his name with-out his okay. Lindsay got arrested at the Gold Nugget's works on Squaw Creek. I ain't one to toss rocks, but fellers what deal with Roller and Twitchell always seem to get the short end of the stick. Slicker than snot on a door-knob those 2 seem to me.

~

Mrs. Jack Williams got the measles.

~

Marshal Stingley got a pound full of stray stock now that he enforcing the ordinance against live-stock roaming the streets.

~

The old Bank Exchange Saloon been spruced up and looks better than ever.

~

There a bunch of childrens running the streets what ought to be in school. Wish the Marshal were as force-ful keeping them snot-nosed little ones where they belong as chasing us drunks from the road.

May 19, 1882
All the sick-ness got doctors running to Salida fast as law-yers after a train wreck. Got us 7 full-time docs here now.

~

Good days be here. Got us another saloon. What with all the law-yers and money men rushing in it be good to have plenty of places to drink. Clemens and Watson opened a saloon in one of J.B. Browne's buildings, opposite the Mandeville Grocery on First.

~

Mr. McPeters putting up a 18 by 20 frame building on F Street across the alley from Webb and Corbin. Gonna sell vegetables. Them boys be running him out of business fast, I guaran-damn-tee you.

~

Got us 10 passenger trains coming and going every day now. Feller can't get a proper nap no matter the time.

May 20, 1882
Jack McCall changed his place so much you won't recognize it. Walls got new paper, ceilings raised 2 feet, the bar got moved to other side of the room, the room moved back a few feet, and he hung lots of hand-some pictures on the walls. As neat a place as you find in town.

~

J.E. Morrison, feller what own the black-smith and wagon shop on Second and E, made a wagon for Max Dickman. Brother, that be one excellent piece of workman-ship. Made it for hauling logs and lumber. Says it hold 6 tons and can pull any-where a team can get.

May 21, 1882
   Salida bursting with prospectors. Fellers what got horses and pack animals to let getting rich for sure. More new faces in town every damn day.

~

   Dickman's Opera House looking a sight better since they added on a balcony.

~

   Stingley on the war-path against strays. Says folks best pay their dog taxes or say good-bye to them. Amen, I says.

~

   Spring sure make some pretty sights. The prairie covered in so many white blossoms it look like snow. Ain't life some-thing?

May 24, 1882
   City got a contract done for the new school-house. Thomas to frame and George W. Bower to build. $3000.

~

   Dr. Gordon already sold the Clarendon Restaurant. Seems doctoring a might easier than feeding folks.

~

   Milk down to 10 cents a quart. Got lots of competition now so's prices better.

~

   Feller name A.T. Johnson, from Kansas and the Indian Territory, opening a tailor shop.

~

   I swear J.P. Smith a great story-teller. He told a tale about a bear what takes the cake. Says a man were out hunting and came across a bear. The bear took off after the feller, so he drops his gun and runs up a tree. Smith says the bear picked up the gun and shot at the man. Only reason the bear didn't load up and fire again is the feller took the cartridges up the tree with him. Smith sure know how to make a feller laugh.

May 26, 1882
   Got us a prize soap man in town, name Soapy Smith, what been shooting off his mouth promiscuously the last 2 evenings. Ain't no-thing but a grand swindle. He has a wheel of fortune in connection with his scam. He gives away a hundred dollars in a horn. He got several steerers on the out-side to bring in the greenies. It a pretty slick game. He opens a big ole suit-case and sets it on a box. Stars off selling fancy soap what get rid of stain and such. When he gots a crowd the con starts. He make a big show of wrapping cash money around soap and wrapping the soap in colored paper. Some ain't got no-thing. He mix 'em all up and offer to sell a bar for $20 with hopes a feller could win $100. When theys no

takers he lowers price to $10. That's when his ringer walks up and buys a bar, and low-and-behold the feller wins big. Then the flies rush to the stink. Course no one wins no-thing. Kind of fun for us old-timers to watch the tender-foots get taken. You see it, and you don't see it, as the saying goes. But people like to be humbugged. Just human nature. If not for that he be run out of town fast. But he ain't.

~

Salida Mining and Milling Company opening soon one-half mile up-river on the east. Assesor Hill says the property worth $245,000.

~

2 damn inches of snow on the ground to-day.

~

obinson's Big Show Circus be here June 21.

~

Business ain't never been so good, folks here say. In 2 years, we gone from a lil rail-road station to a lively town. Betwixt the rail-road traffic and jobbing trade with mining camps, money flowing thru here like dung thru a pig. Now theys found minerals nearby, money men gonna come running to Salida. Won't be long until we gots brick and stone mansions and fancy buildings instead of the shacks what be here now.

May 29, 1882
Mrs. Jennie Wells opened her new place, Delmonico Restaurant, on First Street.

~

The new county hospital looming up in the south-west part of town.

~

I'm feeling sicker than a feller what ate bad eggs. Another damn law-yer thinking of heading here. C.W. Blackmer of Bonanza says he might open in Salida. Lawy-yers, real estate agents, and bankers be the death of us yet.

~

Salida the hot place in these parts for sure. Mr. Douglas of Alpine in town, talking of moving his drug store from there to here.

~

Charles Phillips were before Judge Bowne on drunk and disorderly. $5 fine.

~

Police busy trying to rid town of vagrants and sneak thieves. Weren't long ago theys happy for any-one what spent cash. Now the money folks here, theys particular on who take residence.

~

The shooting gallery the busiest place in town. I re-member when fellers figured who were the best shot by who brought game back from the hills.

~

Theys 60 men on the pay-roll now down at the round-house and repair shop.

JAMES WEST
RETAIL GROCERIES,
A FULL LINE OF ALL STANDARD GOODS.
COR. F AND SECOND ST'S.
SALIDA - - - COLORADO.

Advertisement from The Mountain Mail, 1882

CHAPTER SIX
June, 1882

June 1, 1882
Jack Williams opened a picture gallery and pawn-shop. Strange businesses to put to-gether if'n they ask me, which they didn't.

~

I heard John Robinson's Big Show gonna have the world's only white hippo which cost $10,000. Also, has 70 men and 20 women horse riders and 150 novelties and feats. I heard about this feller, one they call Uncle John Robinson. Folks what know says ain't no show like his any-where. They says the street pro-cession alone worth waking up for. Saving up my money for this one.

~

Max Dickman moving to a new office in his Opera House.

~

Engine Number 40, what were wrecked by the mines, in town for $500 in repairs.

~

I heard the Sheriff joking he down-right bored as'n there ain't been a man shot in the county since dinner. This county getting knowed for killings, that's for damn sure. I keeps my head turning when out and about.

~

John Taylor fined $5 for drunk and disorderly.

~

Andy Butts and a feller name Morgan, his brother-in-law, had a round-up. They both used to work at one of the iron mines near the head of the Ute Trail. Butts lives in a shanty near the depot.
Sun-day, Morgan, who were traveling through the country, got in-vited to Butts for dinner. They got to arguing over some-thing what happened when theys worked at the mines. Of course, they both been drinking. Butts called Morgan a liar. Morgan says if he weren't in Butts house they'd have a problem. Butts told Morgan to get the hell out of his place. Morgan started out of the house when Butts took 2 shots at him. Morgan took off out of the house running around the corner to get away. As Morgan came around the other side, Butts came out the door with his re-volver in hand. Morgan pulled his own re-volver and fired, hitting Butt in the thigh, breaking the bone. Morgan got tossed in jail but Butts weren't up to filing charges, says he started it, and the matter were dropped. Now that's what you call family.

June 2, 1882
J.H. Stewart bought Uncle Dave's Saloon and fixing it up.

Miss T.H. Reed rented a room over Twitchell and Roller's for a millinery and dress-making shop. She gonna live there, too.

Folks complaining some-one throwing rocks at houses at night. My bet be it all them new damn law-yers trying to stir up business.

I heared that Zela the human cannon-ball gonna be part of the Robinson Big Show.

Man named Wilson kilt a feller name Vernon over to Maysville. Cow-boys come riding in-to Salida for revenge, but Sheriff Mix got Wilson under guard at his house, and that were that.

June 3, 1882
I more excited than a virgin's first time at a whore house. The circus, Robinson Big Show, got posters all over town. Theys bringing a $20,000 drove of animals what called kangaroos, a $40,000 critter called a double-horned rhinoceros, a museum, a menagerie, 3 rings, and it taking 50 train cars for the whole show to get to town. Such doings!

Photo-grapher moved in-to a tent a block above the Opera House.

Knight of Pythias organized here. Calling it Iron Mountain Lodge number 19. 25 big-wigs from Salida joined right away. Theys ordered uniforms and regalia and gonna have a big ole ball on July 4 to celebrate.

Daniel Cronin, teamster for Max Dickman, got kicked by a horse with both legs. Broke his arm betwixt the elbow and shoulder, and bruised his back, but he gonna heal. Dr. Stuart set the arm.

Webb and Corbin moving up in the world. Gonna re-place their frame building with a brick structure 2-stories high. 30 feet by 60 feet.

Baxter Stingley got a raise. Making $75 a month now as Marshal. Still ain't near enough for what the job be.

With all the sick-ness in town, Salida paid George Bateman to build a pest house. Cost $20.

June 4, 1882
Denver and Rio Grande were granted a right-of-way on Fourth Street and I Street to put in tracks.

New news-paper fellers coming here. H.C. Brown and E.M. Pelton moving the Maysville Miner office to Salida for a Democratic news-paper.

A.C. Bartlett opened a shoe-maker shop opposite the post office. Might have to give him a visit. It been a long time since my toes ain't feeled the air.

~

Damn rail-road fellers ain't got a lick of sense. For cussedness or the fun of it, a engineer blew his whistle whiles a man were driving his wife and child on the wagon road near the river. The rig belonged to A.T. Ryan. The whistle scared the religion out of the horses, and they wheeled around, throwing them folks in-to the river. The buggy were badly damaged, and both horses hurt badly. The folks weren't hurt none.

June 6, 1882
I declare Joseph Anderson the best jumper in town. Watched him leap over Chris Laub's bar. I seen it with my own eyes.

~

Webb and Corbin got a brand new delivery rig. Wagon double-springed with back action and a broad gauge and the team is a couple of buckskin Norma's with silver mane and tail.

~

Mr. McGuire caught a tarantula spider in back of Alger's Drug Store. I shit you not. He saw a little girl playing with it and grabbed it up.

~

H.C. Pomeroy opened a store for fruit, confections, and notions opposite the Opera House.

~

Master Mechanic Jones says his pay-roll got 160 men including engineers, fire-men, work-men in shops. $11,280 a month. 140 of 'em living here in Salida.

~

George Chedell's wife died at her home. Been ill past 3 months. Left 2 daughters behind.

~

Town board met to pay some bills. $22 to Roller and Twitchell for a coffin and burial of a pauper, 75 cents to Wollman for stationary, $56.25 to Lahr for survey work on water-works, $7 to M.J. Anderson for hauling invalids to the pest house, $35 to D.E. Kelsey to rent his ditch for May, $75 to Marshal Stingley, $15.75 to Mrs. Bender for boarding prisoners, S.H. Phillips got $3 to dig pauper graves, T. Fielding got $7 for room rent for fire apparatus, John Trasay paid $7.50 for work on streets, $25.76 to Wilson Brothers for groceries for pest house, $150 to Dr. F.P. Brown for medical work on the small-pox patients.

Plat of Blake and Westerfield's addition to town were placed on record.

June 10, 1882

George Stingley, relative of the Marshal, in town from Missouri.

~

Max Dickman thinking of turning the Opera House in-to a hotel.

~

Fellers saying we needs a brass band in town. Corbin be a good leader as'n he plays snare drum.

~

Roller and Twitchell says demand for houses ain't stopping. So why the hell don't some-one put up a dozen or so for rent?

~

Uncle Dave Shobe, feller what sold out his saloon, opened a carpenter shop in the rear of Dickman's lumber yard.

Arkansas Valley near Salida, 1880s

June 11, 1882

.I. Ogden bought Gessert's bakery and restaurant. Gonna open a hotel called the Ogden House.

~

The town board made a ordinance to build side-walks on parts of Front, First, and F Street. Theys shoulda said to tear down some of the shabby ones already in town. Feller can loose a team of horses in some of them holes, or at least break a leg if'n walking with-out looking down. Just to-day, I seen 2 ladies passing Blake's corner who fell. Dry goods was scattered, clothes torn, and arms and legs bruised.

Mr. Howell, the jeweler, moved to a new place next door to the post office. It larger so's he can carry more stock.

June 15, 1882
Marshal Stingley and police-man Modie says a gang of confidence man in town. They says the gang best get to walking while the walking still good.

~

Masons talking of putting a lodge in Salida. Says they gonna build a third story on a brick business block what gonna be built this summer.

~

A 16-year-old boy, son of Mr. Campbell of Iowa, broke his leg when a horse fell on it. He were only visiting town. Dr. Stuart set it.

~

Rail-road boys setting up a game of base-ball Sunday. Laid out a field south of town. Sound like good fun to watch. My old bones most likely snap off if'n I tried to play.

~

It the season for broke legs. William Goring, what work for Dickman, fell off his horse, and the horse stepped on him. Broke his leg in 3 places.

~

Got plenty of fresh vegetables in town. With all these new stores, prices down-right proper for working fellers.

~

J.D. Baxter, feller what own the shooting gallery, putting up a bowling alley. We got a bunch more entertain-ment than a few years ago when it weren't no-thing but whores and saloons to kill the time.

June 16, 1882
Webb and Corbin operating out of the Opera House while's building their new brick place.

~

Roller and Twitchell sold their furniture business to Julius Ruff. Theys gonna focus on insurance, real estate, and mining. Ain't like they not wealthy enough as is. Says they soon building a brick building in center of town on First Street and F.

June 20, 1882
Got a traveling dramatic company giving shows for 3 nights over to Dickman's Opera House.

~

Marshal says the pick-pockets what came to town for the circus ain't done well at all.

~

Theys a new poll tax but only 3 of 50 showed up to pay. Stingley going after the rest.

~

Got a new drug store, Douglas and Andrew. Them 2 some enterprising young men.

~

John Watt, section boss for the rail-road, had a party the other night. 40 of us showed up. Had refresh-ments at mid-night, cake, and ice cream. Feller know how to entertain.

June 21, 1882
Seen a bunch of little boys throwing stones down the stove-pipe into Craig's cellar ware-house. Theys gonna be walking stiff if'n Craig sees 'em.

~

Folks planning on shooting fire-works in the park for July 4 but needs to get to work clearing space. Too many dang cactus there. If'n they aren't careful the whole town be a fire-work.

~

John Kelley were drunk and disorderly. Got lodged in the calaboose before Judge Bowne fined him $5. He ain't got no money, so's they put a ball and chain on his foot and put him to work. Kelley ain't liked that none at all. Picked up the ball, went down to the bridge, and jumped off, landing on a island. Hid his-self in the brush. Police-man Modie found him. Now Kelley ain't working. He just sitting in jail with no-thing but bread and water.

~

Mr. Chapman, super-intendent of bridges and roads for the Denver and Rio Grande Rail-road, says he got orders to expand the round-house and prepare for a stone hotel and eating place just north of the depot plus to make the depot larger. Them rail fellers got big plans for Salida.

June 23, 1882
George Stratton one of those toney kind of gamblers who travel on their shape. He were at Stewart's Saloon when Teddy Rowe were setting 'em up. Teddy threw 6 bits on the counter, and whiles the bar-keeps back were turned Stratton gobbled up 50 cents. The bar-keep tolt Teddy he ain't set down enough money to pay for what was called, so Teddy planked down more cash. Drunk fellers be stupid that way. Some-one, might have been me, tolt the bar keep that Stratton scraped off Teddy's funds. The bar keep followed Stratton out-side and boned him up. Stratton pulled a gun and threatened all sort of things. Got arrested and fined $10.

~

Salida barely escaped a disastrous conflagration the other night. This the third or fourth time we been so lucky. Around 10 at night, Sam

Sandusky, feller what clerk for Craig Brothers and sleep in the back of their store, went out-side to the rear, as he do every night, to see if every-thing okay. He seen smoke rushing out the ware-house door which be dug out in the rear of the place. He took to shouting and alarming, and folks come running. Damage from fire and water betwixt $500 and $1000.

Seems the fire weren't no accident but were malicious set. Some-one dropped fire through the stove pipe, the one them little boys tossing rocks down. I think it were fire-crackers, as them boys took to tossing some around town instead of rocks of late. I knowed Mr. Craig chased a few of them little snot lickers away for just such doings.

They ain't had no insurance on the goods.

June 25, 1882
Now that he gots the streets clean, Stingley asking folks to clean up their back yards.

~

Remember Jacobsen, strange feller what called his-self King of Sweden? I heard he got locked up in Denver for 6 months. Poor, odd fellow.

~

Marshall sent 2 vagrants from town. Says others soon to get the boot.

~

What they got going on at Alger's Drug Store? He caught a centipede in his wife's shawl. Got it in a bottle for folks to see.

~

Still gots hundreds of stray dogs growling and nipping in town. Wish the Marshal were as hot to get rid of them as he is us drunks.

June 26, 1882
I heard business fellers wondering why some-one don't start a street sprinkling cart to keep the dust down in town.

~

Webb and Corbin are go-getters. Got 'a list of items for sale what be delivered to every home. Order taker come by every morning to take the list, fill it, and deliver back.

~

Farmers moaning that worms ate acres and acres of peas.

~

Rail-road building small stock-yards 100 yards above the depot. Town gonna reek of cow droppings soon.

~

Salida's base-ball team challenged Buena Vista for a July 4 game, but them boys says they got other commitments.

June 30, 1882
Town selling rights to re-freshment stands at the park for July 4. Cost $10 but only 2-3 getting sold. Marshal to collect and run off any others. City planned on having the Canon City band play, but theys busy. Instead, got the Williams Theater Company band to play that day and at the Knights of Pythias ball that night. Gonna shoot fire-works from the summit of Lookout Mountain. Fellers ain't gonna be sleeping none that day, as'n the morning to
start with cannonading. My head hurts already.

~

Woolman got married. We all thought the news were a joke, but it weren't. He hitched up to Miss Fannie Seely, young lady well known and liked by most.

ALL THE WORLD CONTRIBUTES!

The Monster Mastodon is Coming!

Salida, WEDNESDAY, June 21.

OLD JOHN ROBINSON'S

Overtowering, Gigantic

UNION OF SHOWS!

Great World's Exposition, Menagerie, Aquarium, Museum, Egyptian Caravan

AND STRICTLY MORAL CIRCUS

Which has so outgrown itself as to require

3 Seperate and Distinct Rings

To give its One Hundred and Fifty Novel Specialties and Sensational Performances in the same given time that ordinary Shows occupy in giving but a single performance, in fact, nine hours of entertainment condensed into three.

TEN EXHIBITIONS COMBINED

In one vast village of Colossal Tents, representing an outlay of

TWO MILLION DOLLARs!

A proud monument of successful enterprise, based upon a life-long fidelity to the promises made to the public each season during over fifty years.

It is coming on its own special train of

FIFTY MAGNIFICENT PALACE CARS!

Mr. Robinson has called to his aid, and engaged at a princely salary, the original, veritable and only world-famous veteran,

MR. DAN RICE.

A FEW OF THE MANY

FEATURES AND NOVELTIES:

$45,000 drove of real, live GIRAFFES. Only drove ever on exhibition.
$30,000 drove of White and Black African OSTRICHES.
$20,000 invested in a school of SEA LIONS.
$10,000 drove of Australian KANGAROOS.
$40,000 Two-horned RHINOCEROS, seven feet high; weighs 9,000 pounds.
$10,000 pair of TAMINOURS, from the river Amazon.
100 SHETLAND PONIES, many no larger than a Newfoundland dog.
A drove of ELEPHANTS, among them the aged "EMPRESS," reputed to be 143 years old, certainly the oldest Elephant on record.
The GIANT OX, larger than an Elephant.
$5,000 flock of African Blood-sucking VAMPIRES, that live on nothing but human blood.
$3,000 Man-eating Equestrian GORILLA.
$10,000 White Nile HIPPOPOTAMUS.
$5,000 Royal YAK, from Tartary.
$3,000 Sahara ELAND.
$3,000 African HARTBEEST.
VALPUS, Part Horse and part Cow. Its like has never been seen before.
African POTICHAIN, the only one in America.
Pair of Sacred White PEAFOWLS, from India.
300 yards of African BOA CONSTRICTORS.
A Menagerie of Fifty Dens of rare and costly animals.
Robert Stickney, the only universal Genius of the Ring.
Miss Emma Lake, the most talented and finished Equestrienne in the profession.
Miss Minnie Marks, a brilliant and bewitching Trick Rider.
Miss Christine Stickney, the dashing and fearless four-horse bareback rider.
John Lowlow, the funniest clown and wit that ever cracked a joke.
William Ash, the drollest of humorists.
George Holland, champion bareback and somersault rider.
Edward Holland, a marvelous performer, in wonderful feats with the magic cross and enchanted barrels.
Alfredo Family, performing on a bicycle upon a slender wire elevated above the multitude.
Zula, the human female cannon ball, shot from a huge cannon loaded with real powder.
George Rodgers, the anatomical wonder.
John Barry, in his unequaled bareback somersault act.
Miss Belden, the greatest female solo cornetist.
Miss Lawlaw, the woman of the iron jaw.
James Shultz, the modern Hercules.
Basso and Debuque, gymnasts, in their perilous and thrilling mid air act.
George Scott and family, gymnasts extraordinary.
Klotze, the greatest of acrobatic jugglers.
Eleine, high, long and lightning leaper.
Prof. Samuels' school of comic monkeys, dogs, goats and ponies.

THE NIGHT IS TURNED INTO DAY.

The vast Pavilions of this enormous institution are lighted each night by the world-renowned scientific miracle,

The Brush Electric Light,

The brilliancy of which rivals the dazzling rays of the mid-day sun.

This grand, spectacular holiday street pageant will be an acceptable innovation on the old-fashioned show parades of the past. The extended retinue of cages, dens, vans and chariots are masterpieces of the most elaborate workmanship. Every cage is a study in itself. The unique pony chariots, drawn by a hundred Shetland ponies; new and costly dens and lairs; the elephants, camels and dromedaries all elegantly caparisoned; with the splendid retinue of ring horses, ponies, mules, etc. all magnificently costumed; with banners waving, flags and emblems flying, forming together a pageant grand and imposing.

Admission $1. Children under ten years of age 50 cts.

Will exhibit at Buena Vista, Thursday, June 14, Gunnison on Monday and Tuesday, June 19 and 20.

Advertisements from The Mountain Mail, 1882

CHAPTER SEVEN
July, 1882

July 5, 1882
    Had a good ole celebration for July 4. Them Williams Theater players weren't good tho, and too proud of their value. Theys too expensive and rude to boot, and the town refused to pay. Had 600-700 folks in the grove. Fire-works from the mountain were beauty-ful. Knights of Pythias post-poned their ball on account of the band weren't worth hiring. Some folks took the train to Marshall Pass to celebrate. Only trouble in town were 2 fellers fighting over a gambling debt but weren't no damage other than busted noses and bruised craniums.

~

    Work be done soon on the school-house foundation.

~

    Theys talk again of building a large, first-class hotel in town. Been talk of such from day 1.

~

    Workers excavating yet another new round-house. Gonna be on the west side of the river by the Gunnison track if'n it get built.

~

    Watched Joe Bender whack a feller in a fight at his place. Hit him right on the sconce.

~

    Mr. McGuire kicked a feller out of his Junction House Hotel on account of the man were shouting foul and insulting words.

July 6, 1882
    Marshal says this the last chance to pay the dog license before he starts shooting 'em. Ain't a good time to be a dog.

~

    The wagon road on the south side of the river washed away with heavy rains. Tracks got damaged betwixt here and Nathrop from all the water, and now most lines running late. We all thought the bridge were gonna go, too. It ain't.

~

    J. Eaton drunk and disorderly. Fined $5 plus costs.

~

    Knights of Pythias finally had their ball. 50 couples is said to have showed. I ain't no couple nor society folk, so ain't got no invite. The Knights were said to be showy in their new uniforms. Dinner were served at Delmonico's and the Ogden House.

~

McGuire had some strange doings at Junction House of late. The other day, a man and woman checked in, registered as McNeil and wife. Left the next morning for Gunnison. The cook at Junction House told McGuire the women were actually his wife and wants the marshall to arrest 'em. Gunnison sheriff to prosecute for bigamy or adultery.

~

The Presybterian church voted to invite Reverend H. M. Whaling to take charge for the next year. He accepted, and now gonna be the regular pastor. He a young man. Folks from where he preached be-fore says he got considerable talent and were well-liked and a gentleman. He gots a family, wife, and a child what gonna join him soon.

July 7, 1882

This town got shook up proper the other day. Quarter past 2, folks on First Street, betwixt E and F, got scared with the crashing of timbers as if a building were being torn down. Noise got caused by a run-away team trying to get through Miss Holderby's millinery and dress-making shop.

Edward Ellis, driver for Max Dickman, were loading a lumber wagon near Second Street. The team were left with-out being hitched, a damn foolish thing to do. The noise of the rattling lumber scared the tar out of 'em, and away they went. The horses circled partly around a couple of blocks. When they tried to run back in-to the lumber yard, which sit betwixt Miss Holderby's place and Dickman's old office, they ran in-to one of the gates which were partly open. That threw them against the front of the millinery, and brought the whole matter to a stand-still. Only damage were some broken glass. The ladies weren't even hardly scared.

~

Got house-breakers in town. The assay office with the Salida Mining and Milling company got broke in. Thieves took $200 of money and goods. Professor Meyer and Mr. Holbrook and Mr. Griggs sleeps in the building, but were gone. Holbrook come back and found a window broke and property strewn all over. He says he think he scared 'em off when un-locking the door, as'n a gold watch and chain, worth $100, were left sitting in the open.

~

Don't this beat all? A madam what runs whores, name Lillian A. Browne, suing the managers of Knights of Pythias, including Max Dickman, J.W. Williams, O.V. Wilson. She asking for $20,000 on account of that group ain't let Browne attend their ball the other night cuz they says she ain't no decent nor respect-able person. Wonder if'n any of them fellers ever visited her girls?

~

Stingley says it the last chance for folks to pay the dog tax, or their pups gonna get slaughtered instantly and with-out mercy. Says there ain't no more delays.

~

Feller with quite a reputation, name of Doc Holliday, late of Arizona, in town with 2 other fellers, Osgood and Robinson. They plan to stay a few days. Law in Arizona been trying to get Holiday back to that territory on charges of murder, from a shoot-out there, but Colorado Governor Pitkin refused to honor their requisition. I heard tale Holliday came to Salida after meeting with his friend, Wyatt Earp, over to Gunnison, but folks tell lots of tales when the hour gets late and the liquor gets low.

July 8, 1882

Theys a meeting amongst business owners Saturday talking about a board of trade or commercial union. Gonna get together in the store room recent vacated by N.E. Woolman.

~

Mike Coley drunk and disorderly.

~

Ex-Governor Gilpin coming to town Thursday.

~

Boys at tele-graph office poking fun at Swester cuz he gots a new coat. Ain't never had no new clothes but wouldn't minding getting funned over such.

~

Theys a scheme afoot to build a national bank in Salida.

July 10, 1882

The new Webb and Corbin building gots doors, window caps, and sills coming from Canon City. Mighty hand-some and gonna set the building off in good shape.

~

D.E. Kelsey contracted to build addition on rear of *The Mountain Mail* building.

~

J.W. Strayer of Kansas City visiting. Thinking of building a addition north of town with Charles Van Every.

~

Tuesday night, Mr. Yoakum heard a noise about his chicken house. He investigated and saw what look to be a man. Yoakum let fly with his gun 2 or 3 times, and the what-ever it was fairly set the ground on fire to escape. Next morning, tracks made by a high-heeled boot were discovered. Justice Garrison says only cow-boys and darkies wear such, so seems one of them types was after Yoakum's chickens.

July 12, 1882

Deputy Sheriff from Leadville were in town with a prisoner, and took to complaining about Salida. Says he were imposed on. Says our calaboose ain't safe, so's he wanted some-one to guard his prisoner during the night. Next morning, feller what did the guarding want $10 which the deputy thought were pricey. Theys settled at $7.50, but deputy felt took.

~

Tues-day evening, the train from Gunnison brought Mr. M.E. Hall, his wife, and her sister. He a harness maker fro Kansas who come out this way on account of his wife ailing with consumption. The new air helped for a while, but the sick-ness took over. They were heading back to Kansas so's she could die amongst friends, but she took her last breath at Junction House at half-past 12 noon.

July 14, 1882
Re-member the cook at Junction House what says the man McNeil checked in with the cooks wife? That matter ain't done. The woman, Alfreta Yahr, got brought to Salida from Gunnison on charges of adultery. The woman says she were the cooks wife at one time, but ain't no more. She says he read her a tele-graph what says he filed for divorce, and it were granted. Says she weren't shacking up with McNeil, but were headed to Lake City to work in a hotel. Seems mightly peculiar, but it still going to court.

~

Some of the society-type says Salida need a reading room.

~

Wonder why the city ain't grading F Street from First to Second with the dirt they taking from Webb and Corbin's cellar? Would sure level things out.

~

Lordy, but alleys stinking like a carcass. How folks stand such nasty-ness? Ain't they got sense to bury or burn instead of tossing?

~

Theys a lot of tongue-waging from busy-bodies in this town, but there a few respectable ladies around. Not many, but a few.

~

3 business fellers says they put up $2000 each for a first-class hotel if 9 others can be found. I ain't gonna be 1 of that group that's for damn sure.

~

Theys lots of work to be had shoveling for the new round-house. I ain't open to such sweating work. Seems I ain't alone as the rail-road says they ain't near enough workers in town.

July 17, 1882
Richardson, the side-walk contractor, starting on up-grades.

~

Small group of Italians made it to town to work on the round-house. Says more to come.

~

From the amount of law-suits in Salida you'd think we was the capital of Chaffee County. Too many law-yers here. Ain't no-thing but trouble.

~

Gentleman from Kansas name Metcalf in town looking for work as a teacher.

July 19, 1882
Monday evening a tele-graph came for Deputy Sheriff Mix from Under Sheriff Paint, in Buena Vista, says to watch for and arrest a man what stole a horse up the river. Mix had police-man Modie look out after getting a description of the horse. Horse were found in Ryan's livery stable, and the man were found in a dance hall and locked up in the quay. Later that night, feller what claim to be a partner of the man locked up told Modie he knew the feller be innocent. Modie says, "Perhaps you are the man I want, so I'll put you in the cooler, too." When Modie asked the man his name, he says, "Do you want my Colorado name or my right name?" Says he called Terry. Officer from Lake County came down the next day and took the man back.

~

Salida growing so fast theys already talk of adding a second story to the school-house being built. Would cost another $3,000. They says we gots 235 children school age, but the place being built only holds 120. Course, the place going up weren't de-signed to hold a second story so it won't work like that.

~

What become of the Buena Vista base-ball club? Were it dis-banded? Or they afraid to go against some good players? Salida club sent them a challenge last Monday, but ain't got no reply. If they afraid to face our boys they should own up like men.

~

Ain't no-thing do my body better than watching law-yers lose their cool. Had a case in Justice Bowne's court. Mayor Wilson represented Wilson Brothers. Mrs. Jennie Wells were de-fendant. Theys asked to move things to Justice Garrison's court. While Bowne were making out the papers, an altercation of words broke out betwixt Wilson and Mrs. Wells law-yer, Mr. Starbird.

Bowne kept 'em quiet a bit, but things split on-to the side-walk. Them 2 air-bags engaged in enough words to fill a number of books. If'n words be blows them 2 would have filt the streets with blood, but as it were they ain't done no-thing but suck air from the rest of us.

July 23, 1882
Gots a bunch of folks want to spend their days with childrens. 30 applied for the teaching position. Can't under-stand such.

~

The Ute Trail wagon road in terrible condition. County needs to do some repairs.

~

Marshal Stingley seeking out every-one what carries concealed weapons. Says he gonna pull every mother's son he finds and he means it.

~

Got 30 men working on the water-works. Gonna have flowing water in town before long, and that mighty fine. Beats toting it from the river or well.

~

George Smith's new sign over his business almost large as a meeting house. He down-right serious about folks taking notice.

July 26, 1882
New tracks being laid between the main track and the hills east of the depot.

~

Rail-road bunch of busy fellers. Theys planning a new freight depot north of the passenger depot.

~

I swear some fellers big on talk. John Magher says if Murphy, feller what got only one eye, hits him again it won't be healthy for him. Why the hell ain't Magher knock the stuffing out of Murphy the first time? Then there ain't no problem to talk about.

~

Well, hell. Now a feller can't bath in the river with-out worry. Dr. O'Connor says the likely-hood of catching typhoid fever be high in the bottoms on the east side of the river if'n some-one don't clean up the dirty water and do some-thing about the stagnant water.

July 27, 1882
Buena Vista base-ball club coming up Sunday to play the local boys. Says they ain't got the last invite. I take a feller on his word, but seems odd to me.

~

Gots so much mail coming in now theys carry it by burro from the depot to the post office. And not a damn letter in the pile for ole Sam.

~

The offices built on First and F Street by Roller and Twitchell be the noblest in town. Them 2 sits up-stairs all day and looks over every-thing below like kings.

~

Town ordered a hose cart and 1000 feet of hose for the hose company.

~

Richardson got a contract to build a hotel next to the Ogden House. Gonna belong to Sam Davis and be 40 feet by 50, 2 stories high.

July 28, 1882

'Cheap John,' alias of John Pulvermarker from Gothic, Crested Butte, Gunnison, Maysville, Poncha Springs, Buena Vista and Niyarick leased Woolman's old stand (where Lester and Company was gonna open a saloon, but ain't). Says it to be filled with cheap clothings and other goods. John is a rustler and don't you forget it.

~

Mr. Alexander says theys rushing on the water-works and gonna furnish water to Salida in 3 weeks.

~

V.J. Dolezai, feller with the trade of auctioneering, been in town 3 or 4 days as agent for Davies of Leadville, selling un-redeemd pledges and other articles by a chance scheme. It a old envelope game where you give 25 cents to draw a envelope from a box. Then you gives 75 cents more if you take a prize draw. A.L. Andrews, what work in Howell's jewelery, drew a gold watch worth $65. Dolezai swore out a arrest warrant, says Andrews changed numbers after drawing his envelope. Then Dolzai got his-self arrested cuz the State gots a law against lotteries. Ain't life grand when the swindler get swindled?

~

Fellers what went bear hunting come back, but weren't in good shape. Ain't got no bear. A chipmunk were the biggest wild animal they saw. That ain't worried them much, but some-thing else did. Theys headed up the mountains near Dickman's saw-mill where theys cached cigars, beer, and whiskey to re-fresh them-selves. When they got there the cache were looted.

July 29, 1882

Burglars broke into Ruefly's jewelry store the other night and gobbled some of his tools. They broke the front window to get in. Police-man Modie found one of the work drawers near the Shirley house and some of the tools near the round-house. Ruefly lost $10-$15.

~

Police-man Modie says if the feller what held him up Sunday night come around he gonna whack him. It were near mid-night and Modie were meandering to the dance hall to see how things were going when a feller jumped out, and yelled, "Hold up, there!" Jeff Modie belted the man with a right fist, knocking the feller back 17 feet. Before Modie could get his gun out the scoundrel were up and running fast as lightning.

July 30, 1882

Furniture come in for the new school-house.

~

Timbers in place and masons working on Webb and Corbin's new store.

~

Had good attendance at the Salida Hose Company Number 1 meeting to elect fire officers.

~

There were a feller staying at Mandeville's boarding house what flat out disappeared. Mandeville says the man name George H. Peck. 50-years-old, dark of complexion, medium-size, with a full beard. Says he from Kansas and gots a farm there. Feller just up and vanished. Left a saddle, blanket, some clothes, and other things. Mandeville says that shows he ain't left on his own choosing. They was a man in town talk loud of wanting to see Peck gone. Peck says he ain't knowed that man. That man gone too.

WEBB & CORBIN

Wholesale and Retail

GROCERS.

SALIDA, COLO.

Advertisement from The Mountain Mail, 1882

CHAPTER EIGHT
August, 1882

August 8, 1882
Strayer's addition to town done with the survey. It 25 acres northwest of town. 10 blocks, 22 lots.

~

Painters about done with the roof on that county hospital. Theys ordered furniture. It sits south, near the river.

August 19, 1882
Rumor going around a smelter and iron founder coming to town. If'n I had 2 bits for every rumor what ain't come true, I be a wealthy feller, which I ain't.

~

Dang, but Baxer Stingley a busy man. Got named constable on account of ain't no one want the job.

~

That madam, Lillian Browne, selling her piano at raffle over to Clark's Saloon. Cost $2.50 each. What the world coming to when a whore gots to sell her piano? Ain't a good sign, that for damn sure.

August 23, 1882
Ladies Society of the Presbyterian church having a ice cream festival to raise money.

~

Constable J.D. Lester had a round-up with Max Dickman over wages due. Lester were sued on his official bond. Dickman is on Lester's bond, and admitted he owed Lester some money, but proposed holding back until the law-suit were done. Lester went at him, and got arrested for assault and battery. $10 fine from Justice Garrison.

~

The water-works moving fast down F Street.

~

China-man, Sing Lee, headed to China to get his wife. Lordy, next they be making a bunch of yellow babies what be running all over the streets.

~

4 doctors left town the last months. Says folks too damn healthy in Salida.

Advertisement from The Mountain Mail, 1882

CHAPTER NINE
September, 1882

September 4, 1882
E.H. Webb running for State Senate at the county convention. Seem running a grocery ain't enough challenge.

~

I heard People's Bank gonna open next week.

~

The yard at the depot got re-surveyed for a new track and some changes. A few side buildings to be tore down and new track laid.

~

The fire-men having a ball September 15. I be there. Them boys know how to throw a party.

~

I heard a troubling rumor for them what got money, which ain't me. Folks says the Bank of Salida gone broke. Doors opened Monday, but they ain't got no cash to pay out. W.J. Hartzell, manager, gone to Silver Cliff for cash. Tele-graphs says he be back Tuesday, but we shall see.

~

Taconic Dramatic Club from Buena Vista played to a packed house at Dickman's. A good show it were.

September 9, 1882
Bank of Salida still broke. Ain't got no cash at all.

September 10, 1882
Webb and Corbin's place getting plastered. Be open soon.

~

Timbers on the roof of the new school. Theys gonna open when finished.

~

Clark's ten pin alley the most patronized place in town. Folks do like bowling. I gotta say it were surprising fun.

~

Real estate sales slowed a bunch with the bank failure. And it failed for sure.

~

I seen a dead dog a few days in a row betwixt the opera and the new school-house, but ain't no one moving it.

~

Theys stone left all over the streets by the water-works crews, but ain't no one cleaning. Lazy this town be.

~

Tennessee Jubilee Singers coming to Dickman's September 19. Should be some pretty sounds.

~

Rumor again of a fine hotel coming to the depot. Supposed to be the finest in the region. Rail-road leveling ground, but theys been talking on this a long spell.

September 22, 1882

Streets flat out torn up with the new water-works. Can't hardly walk down it.

~

Hose company were practicing, laying out hoses, hooking up to hydrants, and spraying water. Weren't too fast from what I seen. Then again, watching from the saloon I weren't too fast on the draw, neither.

~

First National Bank of Salida coming. Roller, Webb, White, Craig and some others signed up.

~

Banking business shaking up. W.E. Robertson, feller what started Chaffee County Bank when theys only 3 buildings in town and sold to South Arkansas Bank, coming back to start a new Chaffee County Bank.

~

Hawkins Hotel closed. Mr. Waddell, land-lord of New York House, taking over to re-open.

~

Watched 'em test the water-works hydrants. Seen water fly 45-feet high from the hoses, and not one leaky joint. Water coming from the river, a few rods below Ira King's home. Theys built a dam across the river to form back-water. It 290 feet long, 20 feet wide, with wrought iron pipes.

September 26, 1882

Business looking good at the new Chaffee County Bank. The effects of the failed Bank of Salida now in official hands. How the hell do a bank run out of money? Never met a banker yet weren't living high and dressing like a dandy.

~

Odd happenings. Frank Beebe up and disappeared when strangers come to town looking for him.

~

Theys remodeling the depot to put a tele-graph office in the attic.

~

The other evening, the fire alarm were given. The caleboose were burning. Hose company got there in short order and put it out. 2 Italians what was in the caleboose was scared half to death and I don't blame 'em. Seems some damn fool tossed a cigar stub in a pile of trash.

Folks wanting the fire boys to put the hoses to the street to settle the dust.

Big shots bragging that when the water-works finished, and that national bank gets to town, Salida be the most advanced place around.

Had another fire alarm. Gun shots and bells ringing. Weren't nothing but a bon-fire near Hawkins Hotel. The fore-man of the hose company started the fire and gave the alarm to see how fast his boys could move. Ain't what I call funny.

CHAFFEE COUNTY BANK,

SALIDA, COLORADO.

BANKING IN ALL ITS BRANCHES.

Eastern and Foreign Exchange
Bought and Sold.

Highest Price Paid for County Warrants. Money to Loan on Approved Security.

W. E. ROBERTSON, Cashier.

Advertisement from The Mountain Mail, 1882

CHAPTER TEN
October, 1882

October 1, 1882
Dang dust constant when the wind blows. I spitting dirt most the time.

~

Large team of stone-cutters working on stone for the round-house.

~

I heard the Utah extension of the rail moving fast. Soon, people be visiting Salida from the west coast with-out needing to go through Denver.

~

Hunting party done good. Mr. and Mrs. Williams, Mr. and Mrs. Howell, and Mr. Richardson brought in 3 antelope, 54 ducks, and 23 jack-rabbits. That don't include the 14 ducks and 9 rabbits they ate in camp.

~

Butchers dealing in venison now. Hunters bringing in lots. That some good eating.

~

Dr. Nonamaker moving his press to Salida. His Colorado Mining Ledger to be printed here in the old Lady Gay Saloon building above Second Street. Says he keeping the Maysville Mining Leger in Maysville.

October 12, 1882
It time for ole Sam to lay low. We gots typhoid fever in the area. A man laid up at Grand View Hotel with it.

~

Folks saying Salida need a cemetery. As it is, the dead gots to be toted to Poncha Springs or Cleora for burial.

~

I heard that fancy rail-road hotel to have 24 rooms, a office, dining rooms, waiting rooms, kitchen, store-rooms, and gas works. Theys to be rail-road offices nearby.

October 19, 1882
Fellers getting soft it seem to me. Lots of miners coming in to town to hunker down for the winter. Weren't long ago they stay put in a cabin up in the high country.

~

Had 24 men quit work at the round-house on account of the new fore-man what they don't like.

~

I seen 50 men working on the foundation for that new rail-road hotel. Look like it going up for sure this time.

~

They needs a foot-bridge near the round-house. Fellers have to walk near a mile to get around the river as it is now.

~

That Moore feller, what edits *The Mountain Mail*, talked about the war. He a cripple with a damaged arm. Says he were a soldier for the north when it got shot up.

~

I swear, some folks think rules ain't touching them. City council passed a ordinance saying chimney flues gots to be surrounded by brick, but some council members ain't got theirs bricked up.

October 28, 1882

I learnt the city had $9,000 in the failed bank. That's a heap of cash we ain't getting back.

~

Webb and Corbin painting a large sign on the south side of their new building.

~

Streets crowded at night with all them rail workers. A rowdy bunch they be.

~

Ain't a room to be found at tenement houses or boarding houses. Betwixt miners and rail workers things all full for the winter.

~

Gots near 80 students in school. I ain't no teacher but that a bunch of snot lickers for only 1 teacher to handle.

~

I be damn if there ain't a dog fight every hour. Hundreds of dog fights going on and not a thing being done about it by the law. I thought Stingley were gonna start shooting 'em?

Advertisement from The Mountain Mail, 1882

CHAPTER ELEVEN
November, 1882

November 2, 1882
We gots a fire fiend around, setting fire every damn night. Need a night guard less'n this fool burn the town to the ground.

~

Salida now gots 21 saloons, and all seem a thriving business. I doing my part to support 'em.

~

Craig Brothers putting water pipes in their store.

~

I heard town to have 4 brick businesses in the next 30 days.

~

Governor Hunt donated a lot on the corner of F Street and First for the national bank. Ain't that some-thing? Damn money men getting free land and me living in a tent with a mule. Life ain't fair.

November 8, 1882
Stingley estimates there 40,000 dogs in town, and he hopes 39,999 don't pay the taxes.

~

Skating rink opened. Running Wednesday and Sunday nights. I ain't going. I slips enough on ice with-out paying for it.

~

It seems Mr. Crowley took exceptions because Judge Painter were employed as counsel against him in a law-suit. Them 2 run in-to each other at the post office, and Crowley let loose with derogatory remarks on Painter, calling in-to question his parentage, character, personal appearance, color, and more. Fancy with words he was. The Judge took exception to the words and suggested the 2 settle things manly, but only out-side the city limits so's they don't get arrested. That got a crowd gathered. They started marching south with a bunch of fellers following, but time they passed West's Bakery, Crowley weak-end. After a few parting words, the fellers went their own way. A bunch of bluster and hot air it were, but no blood which were down-right disappointing.

November 17, 1882
They says Salida to have 2,500 people here by next year.

~

Young men act down-right silly if'n you ask me. A young Adonis took it on his-self to grab up a fiddle to woo a girl he were sweet on. He wrapped the fiddle in a gunny-sack, went to her home, and positioned his-self under her window to produce Heavenly sounds to win her heart.

The girl's mother had gone to bed and were drifting off to sleep. At the first tortured sound of the boys playing, the mother sat up in bed and screamed, "Robbers!" Her husband bounded to the floor, grabbed a boot jack, threw up the window, and screamed, "Scram, you bitches!" He throwed the boot jack at the boy, hitting him smack dab betwixt the eyes. Well, the howl that boy let out woke half the town. He dropped the fiddle, done a few somersaults in the gravel, and fell over a wood-pile, down-right demoralized. He spit out a mouth-ful of teeth, jumped over a freight wagon, and left fast as a running horse. Poor feller were found in the morning, near froze to death, under a pile of lumber at Dickman's. And folks wonder why I don't give no truck to matters of love. Women ain't no-thing but trouble.

November 18, 1882
James Bathurst now in charge at Jim and Charley's Saloon.

~

Water coming from them new hydrants be rust-colored and taste like barn-yard drainings. Cattle won't even drink it.

~

There were 100 folks at the skate rink last night. 25 had on skates, and Police-man Jeff Modie were one. Hilarious it were watching him. One of his legs visited Pueblo, and the other went to Leadville.

November 19, 1882
Bathurst, feller tending bar at the place next to Devereaux's, had 3 men come in trying to sell him 2 cadies of tobacco. Bathurst didn't buy, as'n he thought some-thing weren't right. Instead, he tolt the Marshal about the 3. Marshal tolt Bathurst a rail car were stole from the night before, and them 3 might be the ones, so Bathurst, being a good feller, found them men and says he want to bargain. Marshal says he be near to watch. Them boys weren't stupid, and smelt a rat. They took off for the hills, but Stingley and Sheriff Mix headed 'em off and tossed 'em all in the cooler. They ain't give names, but one knowed as 'Broken-nose Scotty.' Police-man Modie found 2 cadies of tobacco hid in a rail car the next day.

November 24, 1882
River down way low.

~

Webb and Corbin painted their new store a somber green. They says it don't show dirt like bright colors but gloomy it be.

~

Feller claim to have run in-to a robber what stole from the rooms over Freeman's Restaurants. Turns out he were the robber his-sef. He were working for Mr. Brown, the wood hauler, got paid Saturday evening, robbed the rooms, even went so far as to steal pants from under a sleeping fellers head, packed his kit the next morning, skipped his board bill, and left on the 2 p.m. train. Such be life in the West.

~

Party called on Cheap John Fri-day and bought a fine suit of clothes, and paid with a check. John found it were worth-less, but not until the feller were gone. He swore out a warrant, and Stingley found the man over to Cleora. He got the clothes back, and let the rascal skip.

November 25, 1882
Late Satur-day after-noon, when a freight train came in from the east, rail fellers seen a body of a murdered man laying near the track above Cleora. The news spread with great excite-ment. Mix and Stingley went to the depot, and found a party of men had gone down on a hand-car to bring back the body. What they found weren't no dead body but only a dead drunk.

~

Managers of the new First National Bank of Salida rented the building, safe, and fixtures of the broke bank the Hartzell's owned.

Delmonico Restaurant,

BY

MRS. JENNIE WELLS.

The Delmonico Restaurant is open to the public and is prepared to furnish everything the market affords on short notice.

Give Me A Trial.

First street, Salida, Colorado.

Advertisement from The Mountain Mail, 1882

CHAPTER TWELVE
December, 1882

December 7, 1882
Almost every-body is moaning about the be-fouled condition of the water. Seems it were caused by the action of the Columbus Stamp Mill dumping refuse into the river. Folks can't agree on a remedy. Seems a law-suit needed, but the Columbus company made of power-ful fellers—rail-road magnates and wealthy nabobs from back east.

~

Town board full of thieves in suits, that's for damn sure. They removed Roller as treasurer on account of he kept $650 what weren't his even after theys asked him for it. They says it were il-legal. Them money fellers ain't no-thing but robbers in suits.

~

Lots of new mechanics in town working on the machine shop and round-house.

~

Black Paddy, the rustler, were in the cooler the other day, and got cold. He built a fire in one corner of his cell. Well, ain't no surprise smoke started to issue from the roof and people ran. Black Paddy were rescued only slightly injured, and the fire put out. Damn idiot.

December 10, 1882
Petition going around demanding the city account for finances. Folks ain't trusting a one of the council.

~

Folks had a meeting at Judge Painters place to discuss a library association. Webb got appointed chair-man.

~

Theys putting sky-lights in the depot so's folks can see on gloomy days.

~

Got 7 people in the new county hospital.

~

Lots of men stopped work on the new hotel, and in the rail yards, because the rail-road cut their wage.

December 23, 1882
Betwixt 4 and 5 Sunday morning, Dr. O'Connor got called to visit Kate Armstead's, colored woman what lives in a small house in the rear of the Grand View Hotel. When the doctor got there, Kate were un-conscious. Doctor says it were opium or morphine poisoning. He gave a anti-dote but it ain't worked. 3 that after-noon she were dead.

Bette Ditto, a colored gal, testified to the coroner she were in Kate's company. Bette come from Denver on the 6:40 evening train cuz of letters and tele-graphs from Kate. They knowed each other at Leadville. Bette says she took to using morphine in Denver and brought a bottle with her. Says she put it on the window mantle when she arrived, and told the others it were poison and not to touch it. That night, Kate were up complaining her arm were hurting bad. Bette says she ain't seen Kate take no morphine, but round 4 in the morning, Eva Caitlan, another colored girl who lived with Kate for 3 months, heard Kate breathing so hard it scared her. She tolt Bette that Kate were dying. Bette says Eva tolt her she gave Kate the morphine for her aches and throwed the bottle out. Bette looked for her bottle and didn't find it, so she calls for the doctor. Bette says Eva begged her not to tell the doctor she gave Kate the morphine.

The law ain't believed Bette's story. Theys found a bottle in back of the shanty what read *Sulphate of Morphia,* and thought it the bottle Bette brought from Denver. The coroner jury found a verdict of death by poison by the hand of Bette Ditto. She in jail for trial.

~

One of our fancy business-men were napping when some-one slipped up and relived him of his watch and chain. Watch were second-hand with-out crystal or rim. Chain were nickle plate. I ain't never slept so hard a feller could rob me.

Railroad Saloon

R. DEVEREUX, PROP.

Wines and Liquors OF THE Best Brands. I keep the finest line of cigars to be found in Salida.

Advertisement from The Mountain Mail, 1882

Bird's Eye View of Salida, 1883
Salida Museum Association Collection. Salida Regional Library, Salida, Colorado

JOURNALS

*'Salida Sam' Hayes Journal
Volume 2*

CHAPTER ONE
January, 1883

January 2, 1883
 Carpenters putting finishing touches on the fire bell tower. It gonna look out over all Salida

~

 Went walking down by the round-house. Neighbor-hood what popped up down there busy as a bee-hive.

~

 The coon dive over in the place folks call *soup bone alley* ain't no more. Folks say the morals of Salida better now. Neighbors made a ruckus with the city to get rid of it. Stingley talked to the proprietress of the dive like a Dutch uncle, and suggested they move to a climate more suited to their people. The way the message were gave them darkies took off at once.

~

 Roller and Twitchell dis-solved their partner-ship. Twitchell gonna sell real esate and insurance at the old building. He bought out Roller. Roller bought the furniture business back from Julius Ruff.

~

 F.D. Howell re-tired and F. Heiderhoff took over as publisher of *The Mountain Mail*. He from Leadville.

~

 Corey's Saloon closed.

January 4, 1883
 Late the other night, a professional bad man from Leadville tried to stir up a row in the neighbor-hood by the depot. He were loud, saying he could whip the whole of creation. When he got un-bearable, a rail-road feller took him by the collar, booted him 2 or 3 times, and sent the feller away, sadder but wiser.

~

 All the bakers in town agreed to sell a pound of bread for 5 cents, 2 pounds for 10 cents.

Salida Hose Company Number 1
Frank Thomson Collection, Salida Regional Library, Salida, Colorado

January 7, 1883

I heard a short line rail gonna be running soon from Salida to Denver. Every-one in town counting on getting rich from all the traffic.

~

If'n the good ole days weren't gone before they sure is now. More and more men what own businesses bringing families to town.

~

Theys opened a solid-built foot bridge across the river by the round-house. Foundation made of boulders.

~

The most ferocious looking brute of a dog chained at the rear of the saloon next to *The Mountain Mail* office. Looks like a cross betwixt a bear and a dog, but more like a bear. He came up from Gunnison City where he killed every dog he got hold of until the local authority put a prize on his head. Belongs to a feller name Leonard Kurtz.

January 9, 1883

Rail brake-man, R. Gillip, had a awful accident around 3 p.m. Lost 3 fingers on his right hand. He were coupling a few loaded cars when a big wind come up, blowing smoke in from the coal kiln near-by. It were thick and blinded Gillip and he got his hand caught betwixt the bumper, smashing it to jelly. Theys brought him to Salida, to the Ogden House, where Dr. J.W. O'Connor cut off those 3 fingers. Doc used chloroform, but the feller still suffered greatly. He were a tough one to knock out.

January 10, 1883

Had a peculiar case in town what got folks talking. I don't know what to think on it all. A 15-year-old girl says she got enticed to go up-stairs in a neighbor-hood off the beaten path. 2 women convinced her. The girl says these women drugged her.

The girl's father ain't seen her home after school like she were supposed to, and he went looking. He went to the home of Bill Anderson, the dance hall man what lives up-stairs in Judge Bowne's building. Many times he told his girl not to go there. Seems she weren't good at listening.

The girl came home at 7 that night, staggering and not making sense. The father sent for the doc what says the girl be on morphine. He says the girl told him she were gave the drug by force until she passed out. Anderson gots a different story which ain't no surprise. Anderson says the girl drops by often to visit with him and his wife. He says the girl a wild one, wanting wine, beer and such, and that she gots a un-natural craving for stimulants. That sounds about right to me. This girl ain't no angel from what I heard. Anderson says this teen-ager come over after school and begged for some champagne which he brought from the dance hall. He says the girl drank so much she vomited, and had to lay on the sofa. That's when her father came by. He knowed the girl had a habit of visiting with this couple. Anderson says he ain't told the father the girl were there cuz the man always took to beating the girl with-out mercy when she drank liquor. He says they wanted to save the girl from another beating. When the girl got a bit sober, he says they gave her strong coffee and sent her home. Anderson says weren't no force to it, and the girl drinks often at his place, and be wanting to go to the dance hall, but he and his wife ain't never let her.

January 12, 1883

Got a new news-paper in town, *The Sentinel*. Damn near as many news-papers in Salida as law-yers.

~

Dr. Nonamaker gots pneumonia.

~

A team coming in from Brown's Creek got in-to their heads to run away at the corner off F Street and First. They kept on with their wild ways until coming to Fisher's hay and grain store, where the wagon ran in-to the corner of the building and tore a bit of it out. That ain't slowed them none. The horses went on towards Poncha. Ain't been seen since. For all I know theys down to Saguache by now.

January 15, 1883

Ain't no-one denying the Knights of Pythias ball were the finest Salida ever seen. Theys had visitors from Poncha and Garfield and Maysville. The hall were crowded. Ain't never seen so many ladies dressed fine.

~

Those what weren't dancing at the ball got woke good when the fire alarm went off last night. There was bells, whistles, and pistol shots shouting a fire were going on.

We all ran in-to the road, and seen A.T. Ryan's Livery Stable burning, the one on First Street, north of the rail-road track. Ain't sure how it started, but seem some-one set it. A stable boy were sleeping in the office. Weren't long until the whole place were blazing.

The loco-motives did a good job waking the town. The new little fire-bell, the one in the hose tower, tried hard, but it just too small to be heard.

The hose company boys were on the spot fast, but the fire plugs was 800 feet away, near Mulvany's, so's they weren't much water pressure. Plus, the plug closest, the one by Ogden House, got left open so it won't freeze which made the pressure low, too.

Many of the fire boys had their Knights of Pythis uniforms on, and the fire damaged them so much they ain't use-ful no more. Ryan's building got lost, but them boys saved the one next to it. There was a furious wind blowing, making things even harder. Six horses got burnt and a bunch of buggies.

It were power-ful cold, and some of them fire boys got fingers and ears and noses injured. Them boys was heros all. J.M. Buster stuck with the nozzle until he were covered in ice from head to foot. Had to be taken away by friends and cared for. Charlie Rose got hurt bad too. Craig, Webb, and the Wilson brothers fought hard as did a bunch others.

January 19, 1883

Sam Sandusky, that popular and good-looking clerk for Craig brothers, went east on business and came back with a bride. Good for him. Ain't a proper single gal to be found here.

~

Pay car coming to-morrow with $40,000-$50,000. Town about to be rich.

~

A stranger were talking to the police-man the other day. "Is there any chance in this city to earn a honest living?" he asked. "I don't know," the police-man said, "but we are very progressive and most any experiment is worth trying."

CHAPTER TWO
February, 1883

February 27, 1883
Theys a petition amongst business owners to widen First Street between E and G, to 25 feet.

~

The first folks came to Salida nearly 3 years ago. Got us 3,000 people now. Won't be long until we as big as Denver, and that just sad. Got about 100 businesses to boot. I counted, and we gots 1 bank, 5 hotels, 9 groceries, 3 meat markets, 3 hard-ware stores, 4 dry goods stores, 3 bakeries, 6 restaurants.

~

That nice new foot bridge by the round-house need to get raised by 10 feet or the spring melt gonna wash it out.

~

Got 18 saloons in town now. Each pays $200 a year in license and that's a bunch of money that drunks like me funding.

CHAPTER THREE
March, 1883

March 4, 1883
Windsor Hotel opened. It the largest and best furnished in town, sitting where the old New York House were, on First Street opposite Chaffee County Bank. H.J. Hakins opened it, adding to the Hughes House he moved from Maysville. The Windsor the largest building in town by half. Gots a grand stair-case what opens to the street. Also got a shaving parlor, a reading room with all the daily papers in the State, and a dining room what sits 75.

March 11, 1883
Theys a bunch of cowardly attacks going on. People getting caught un-aware and whacked with bludgeons. I keeping my head turning, I guarantee.

~

We gots 16 passenger trains a day passing through Salida.

~

The fire hose company having a parade and ball March 30.

~

Bickel Brothers opening a shoe- and boot-making place on F Street.

March 14, 1883
They was a big crowd of the smartest, wealthiest men in town at the Opera House to nominate for city officers. The turn-out speak loud about how up-set folks is with the town board.

~

Around 11 last night, the night watch-man seen a fire on the second floor of the new rail-road hotel. He ran for water, but time he got back it were out of control, and he shot his re-volver to sound alarm. The fire boys was coming out from the vote meeting, and were on it fast. They hooked the hose to the plug on F Street and Front, but it were short and could reach only by stretching directly across the river. Time theys figured this out, the fire were pouring out 2 windows and climbing up to the fresh painted roof. Once water was turned on they had it put out fast. I looked at the char after, and were surprised the place got saved at all. Them fire boys fought like giants, and were heros. $3,000 damage.

~

The new rail-road hotel gonna cost $40,000. 10 times what they says it would be.

~

Jake opened a place opposite Webb & Corbin's. Got 5 cent beer, and that sure to get my business.

FIVE CENT BEER!

JAKE'S PLACE,

F Street, opposite Webb & Corbin's. Fresh Beer always on draught. Finest Lunch in the city at

JAKE'S PLACE - - **FIVE CENT BEER.**

Advertisement from The Mountain Mail, 1883

CHAPTER FOUR
April, 1883

April 28, 1883
King of Sweden still in jail in Denver. Poor fellow quite insane.

~

Webb and Corbin selling $1,200-$1,500 of goods daily. Ain't many stores in the State can do that.

~

I swear I don't under-stand folks. City gonna advertise Salida to bring more folks in. Says other cities doing it, and we gonna get left behind if'n we don't. So get left behind, I says! Don't need more damn people. Things already crowded enough.

CHAPTER FIVE
May, 1883

May 3, 1883
New ordinance tells folks to stop re-navigating the irrigation ditches.

~

The new rail-road hotel gots a name now. Called Monte Cristo which means mountain of Christ in Mexican. Ain't never heard the hill behind called such. Some dandy name it I'm guessing. Feller name Harlow gonna manage.

~

H.C. Pomeroy, feller running the fruit store, got appointed police magistrate.

May 10, 1883
The number of buildings being laid out by the rail-road are more than all they got right now. Busy they getting.

~

Town planting trees on Front Street from E Street to G. Says they gonna clear the stones and rubbish from the road to the river. Guess they don't want train visitors seeing un-sightly things.

~

J.S. Painter, law-yer, been in talks with Colorado Telephone Company to connect lines in other cities to Salida as this town gonna be the biggest connection point out-side of Denver. Theys building thousands of miles of lines.

May 30, 1883
If'n folks thought Salida got civil and dandy theys thinking different now. Had us a shoot-out likes of which I ain't never seen. I doubt folks ever for-get this one.
Marshal Stingley, Deputy James Bathurst, and 2 other fellers got gunned down in day-light. I seen it.
Thomas Ninemeyer, a charcoal burner from Brown's Canyon, what works for Millan and McKee, came to town with his father, his brother, Boon, Bill O'Brien, and Tom Evans. They was serious drunk and making violent threats all around. The Marshal and the Deputy took their guns cuz re-volvers and drunks don't make for good company.
Come 6 in the evening, them boys were drunker and was eating dinner at Bender's Hotel. Evans were full of Bender's rot gut, and got to being abusive to the cook and the waiters, and took to yelling for coffee. John Thayer, a rail-road man, told the waiter girls to get out of the way and he'd wait on Evans, which he did. He were taking his seat when the

Marshal and Deputy walked in. That's all it took as'n the situation seems like it were a set up.

Ninemeyer, who ain't said a thing all this time, goes for his re-volver right away. He took to shooting while backing to the door. Evans went at the Marshal with a big knife. He got shot by Deputy Bathurst, and staggered out-side, and died on the side-walk not long after. An old feller, name J.D. Gannon, black-smith for the rail-road, were sitting at a table minding his business. He stood up to get out of the fight and Ninemeyer blasted him in the chest.

Bathurst got shot in the left breast, just below the heart. He ain't likely to survive, the doc says, but he fighting hard.

Stingley got shot in the left groin, the ball passing by his bladder before lodging under the skin on the back-side of his thigh. He also got shot on the left side, where his pocket watch were in his vest pocket. The watch were shot to smithereens, but it slowed the ball enough to save Stingley's life. Punctured a lung, but ain't kilt him yet. Doc says it too soon to know for sure.

Ninemeyer ain't waited to see how things shook out. He took off running west on First Street, towards Devereaux's. I seen Chris Laub and A.T. Ryan try to stop him, and they got shot at for their pains.

A bunch of us took off after Ninemeyer, cuz shooting law-men ain't tolerable no matter the cause or drunken-ness. He run past Ryan's Livery Stable and Moody's Lumber Yard with 50 or 60 of us giving chase. Fellers had what-ever weapon they could grab on the fly, rifles and re-volvers and shot-guns and clubs and knives. Me, I had my re-volver and a knife I keeps handy. We fired and Ninemeyer re-turned the salute which scattered most of us. Talking tough and being tough ain't nearly the same.

Watching the show, a bit down the road, were William H. Brown, a teamster. He borrowed a gun and un-tied one of his horses and gave Ninemeyer a chase. He got with-in a few rods of Ninemeyer, who now were on the mesa north of the rail, not far from William Van Every's home. Ninemeyer, the son-of-a-bitch he be, turned and fired at Brown, killing the man. Then he tried to steal the horse. The horse turns out to be the toughest of the bunch, and ain't put no truck with getting stole. Horse slowed Ninemeyer enough for Ryan, William Goring, and Charlie Rose to catch up and capture the villan.

I ain't gotta tell you that lynching was in the air. Ain't no need for a jury trial on such. His guilt weren't no-thing to argue. Only problem were no man wanted to be the one to lead the crowd in such nefarious doings. Mayor Westerfield and others urged the fellers to let the law handle it proper so's a murder weren't on no-bodies soul. I reckon that were wise, but I sure wanted to see that sorry whore's son swing. I knowed a lot of fellers felt the same.

By 9 that night, Ninemeyer were in Judge Garrison's office, under protection, less'n liquid courage take over and the rope get handed out in sentence by the boys.

I heard that around 11, they sneaked Ninemeyer by wagon to Buena Vista to the county jail.

Charles Ranch Granite Outfitting Shop, Granite, Colorado, 1882
Patricia Bradbuy Holton Collection, Salida Regional Library, Salida, Colorado

CHAPTER SIX
June, 1883

June 1, 1883
Talked to-day with fellers from Brown's Canyon. Seems Ninemeyer and Evans and the gang meant to cause a round-up the other day. Them boys were feared in that town. They says they going hunting, but was stopping in Salida first to clean out the town. They was warned to tread light, but Evans says, "I'd like to see the color of the son-of-a-bitch's face who can arrest me." I'm guessing he seen it al-right.

Them boys was heading here over a grudge Ninemeyer got with the Marshal and Deputy. Seems a few weeks ago, Ninemeyer claim to got robbed by a whore he were sporting with, and the law tells him they can't do no-thing as'n he got no proof and the whore says it weren't true. That ain't sit well with Ninemeyer. He swore revenge, and brother he got it.

June 2, 1883
J.S. Boon swore in as temporary Marshal. Eli Chenoweth as temporary Deputy.

June 4, 1883
I swear some men just contrary to the bone. From day one, I tolt the news-paper feller the name of the publication ain't made no sense at all. What the hell 'mail' gots to do with a news-paper? Well, that feller came up to me today, grining, and says he finally agreed with me. Says he re-named the paper. I picked up a copy, and he were telling the truth. It now called *The Salida Mail*. A son-of-a-bitch he be, but made me laugh loud and long.

~

I be more excited than a tyke waiting on Santy Claus. Heard to-day John Robinson's Big Show bringing 2 ele-phants. That's the truth! Theys straight from dark Africa. Having 'em a parade to boot, plus 3 rings and 90 performers. I guarantee you I be sober for this one.

June 7, 1883
Thomas Ninemeyer, cock-sucker what murdered Deputy Bathurst, Billy Brown, and that black-smith Gannon, on May 30, were brought back to town for what they calls a pre-liminary investigation. He been kept at the county jail in Buena Vista for his health.

At the depot, he were put in a wagon with a heavy guard which were wise. Theys a bunch of us there, and not a word were said. If a feller had started I'm pretty sure the rest of us woulda joined in to lynch the son-of-a-bitch, but no one did no-thing. He were taken to Dickman's Opera House, and we all followed.

The law weren't taking no chances. They had every-one leave their guns to enter. That were wise as'n some-body prolly woulda shot him.

Ninemeyer must got a bunch of money backing him cuz he had a team of law-yers on his team. Judge Rice of Leadville, Ellsworth and Miller of Buena Vista, McDevitt and Lawrence of Salida, and some others were on his side. Prosecuting were J.S. Painter and S.W. Taylor of Salida. Justice H.C. Pomeroy were presiding.

The testy-mony took damn near all day, but ain't no one said no-thing we ain't already knowd.

W.A. Bauslin testy-fied he seen Ninemeyer running up G Street betwixt First and Second, past the black-smith shop where Bauslin works. Then, he seen him run past Moody's lumber yard, down across the rail-road track, and to the mesa near Van Every's home. He talked about Ninemeyer shooting at the crowd what followed. He seen Brown on horse-back get shot when he were with-in 50 feet of Ninemeyer.

Mrs. Sarah Bell testy-fied she seen the same.

L.A. Whitney testy-fied he seen part of the shooting.

Dr. O'Connor says he examined Billy Brown's body, and it were shot on the right side. Says it also shot on the left side about 4 inches from what they call a vertebrate, which mean back-bone in medical talk.

A.T. Ryan says he seen it all, and Ninemeyer fired the last shot when he were by Van Every's potato cellar. When Ninemeyer tried to get on Brown's horse, Ryan says Charley Mullen shot at him, and that stopped it all. Mullen were only 25 or 30 feet away.

W. Rockwell and Dr. Underhill also had a say.

Ellsworth, law-yer for the de-fense, didn't offer no-thing at the time. Mr. Rice, also for de-fense, ain't asked for bail.

The prosecutors says they gonna have other charges to come besides the ones for murder.

~

Folks mighty up-set with the Bender's on account of the murders took place in their place after they served liquor to them boys from Brown's Canyon. But theys were already skunk drunk. Theys a petition about to re-voke Joe Bender's liquor license. Mr. Shaw had a cooler head, and made a motion the matter be in-definitely post-poned, and the others agreed.

~

Town board made new ordinances. One were to cut down on gambling tables in town, and one were to tax all traveling shows.

Both seem a bit rough for my liking, but that's what happens when families and womens make it to town.

~

They was some-thing writ in the news-paper what were so pretty I cut it and made up a paste to stick it in this journal. Some-things can't be made better. It were writ by B.F. Garrison for that Bathurst feller what got murdered last week. They calls it a obituary which mean final words about a feller what died.

A.G. Curtis General Store & Post Office, Granite, Colorado 1880
Patricia Bradbuy Holton Collection, Salida Regional Library, Salida, Colorado

James H. Bathurst.

The last tribute to a good man when his sands of life have ebbed away is but justice to his worth. No marble monument will hardly rise or storied urns record the traits of character that marked his earthly career. I have known poor "Jim" for many years and knew him well, and to know him as I did was to admire him. His exterior was uncouth, his habits were on the order of fun and mirth, his behavior was unceasing gesture and ready repartee, his conduct in relation to all the higher duties and obligations of life, the climax of honor and good faith. In business his word was an early execution of a promise, a promise

> not put aside and never unfulfilled. He was a friend under all circumstances, on all sorts of occasions and in all sorts of ways. He never ceased an untiring and constant devotion to those he loved and admired. His word to a friend was the soul of honor exemplified. His affection and devotion to his little son now in Missouri was the mark of a heart within him possessed of the higher order of parental feeling.
> His love for the wife that survives him was as illimitable as time. His official conduct was guaged by a feeling of sympathy and mercy. His bravery was proverbial with those who knew him, and to his death he marched with unfaltering tread and met it with no emotion of fear or restraint. These words are not unmeaning flattery, but the sincere sentiments of a devoted friend.   B. F. GARRISON.

The Salida Mail, 1883

June 20, 1883

Under Sheriff R.M. Painter arrested Freeman Howell, that colored cook over to the Virginia House, the one on Front Street and F, after he gots a tele-gram from Charles T. Freeman, sheriff of Dayton, Ohio. It says Howell be a accomplice to Dan Harris, and them 2 murdered a feller in 1878. If it true, then Howell's proper name be Harrison Page. Painter sent a photo-graph to that sheriff in Ohio. If'n it the same feller he gonna hang.

~

June 22, 1883
Lord A Mighty, Lord A Mighty, what terrible sad news. Clara M. Roller, lady married to William W. Roller, thems what had the little boy drown? She died. Weren't but 31 years old. Folks saying a broken heart done it.

~

June 27, 1883
Thursday night, John O'Toole, white feller, and George Jones, colored boy, 2 gamblers from over at Del Norte, got into it over a card game. I heard Jones knowed as a bad one back home. But it were just words, and that were that.

Later, they met up in the office of the Virginia Hotel, Front Street and F, each with a gun and each wanting to have at it, and they did so without even a 'How do you do?' to the owner, Mr. Waysman.

O'Toole brought his gun down on Jones head and fired a shot what went right over Jones head. Jones jumped behind the office counter and O'Toole took cover across the room behind the stove. For a few minutes, them 2 had a game of bo-peep with the stove getting the worst of it. O'Toole took off up the stairs, firing one shot from the top, down at Jones.

I swear them boys put a dozen holes in that hotel, but not a damn one in each other.

Officer Stewart showed up and took both men in. Next morning, theys before police magistrate Pomeroy. O'Toole got fined for firing disturbing the peace, and making a im-proper display of a deadly weapon, and he got fined. Jones, that colored feller, were charged with disturbing the peace, and also got fined.

Theys shoulda been charged with being a piss-poor aim and throwed in the calaboose to practice.

CHAPTER SEVEN
July, 1883

July 1, 1883
   Theys put out the program for the July 4 festivities. Ain't a mother's son gonna sleep in that day. Things get started at sun-rise with a firing of guns. Then theys a meeting at the Opera House at 9:30 for a parade with A.T. Ryan the marshal of the day. Ain't that some-thing? He a good man and a good choice. There gonna be choir music, prayer, band music, and a reading of the Declaration of Independence, the paper what says we all free. Of course, gonna have a bunch of poli-ticians speeching, and that prolly go on for hours. At the park, theys a contest betwixt brass bands. Lots of games, too—sack races, burro races, dog races, high jumping, standing jumping, and base-ball at 3:30. They gonna have fire-works at night, then a dance for every-one with the Salida Coronet Band playing. It be a good time for sure.

~

   H.B. Carter opened a ice cream parlor and fresh fruit place on the corner of First Street and F. That there a pleasant treat what shows city life ain't all bad.

July 6, 1883
   I don't know much about college and proper school, and by not much I mean I don't know shit, but theys a big push in town to win a Presbyterian college for Salida. We ain't talking sending childrens to reading and writing school, but a place for what they calls higher education like doctoring and law-yering, God help us all.

~

   S.B. Westerfield's opened 2 doors down from *The Salida Mail*, what used to be *The Mountain Mail*, cuss 'em all.

~

   C.F. Finne, night fore-man at the round-house, laid up with mountain fever.

~

   Trains from Salt Lake City keep coming in late on account of that track in bad shape.

~

   Gots close to 400 childrens in the school now.

~

   Ain't had near the drunk-ness this July 4. Police magistrate Pomeroy thinks the saloons were conspiring against him, says they watered down the drinks. Says he knowed 3 or 4 men what drank all day and got more sober. I weren't one of 'em. I woke with a power-ful head-ache.

~

Remember G.D. Moll, feller what were agent of Gail and Ax, dealers in tobacco and cigars? He were one of the first enterprisers in Salida, always up to some-thing. He the one what fought 1 of his employees, and loved the attention he got for that in the news-paper on account of he seen it as free advertis-ing for his business. This the same feller what buckled up a gun and got lowered in-to the well when theys a dead body at the bottom. Well, he went over to Denver if'n you recall. Been on their police force a while, always in their news-paper for arresting bad men. Now he knowed for some-thing new. Moll got married to a lady name Pauline Peinders from Brooklyn, New York. Getting hitched is a pure act of bravery on his part, and I tips my hat to him.

July 14, 1883

One of them fraternities, called The Masons, had a planning meeting to form a lodge in Salida. Roller, Westerfield, J.H. Moody, A.F. Holland and the other money fellers were part of the group.

~

Town board made a official call to get the Presbyterian college to build in Salida.

~

The Boulan Comedy Company headed this way from Gunnison. Theys bringing jokes, burlesque, fiddle players what they call violinists, which mean music a feller can't dance to, and a bunch of song and dance. News-paper to Gunnison says it a show worth the money.

July 20, 1883

I always says angering a woman the stupid-est thing a feller can do, and that be true. But putting the hurt on a woman's child makes her crazier than a feller 3 days into bottles of rot-gut.

Mrs. Fleck, what runs a restaurant on First Street, were in Grand Junction on business. Whiles she were gone, a feller, one what gonna swing by a rope one day, made a assault on Mrs. Fleck's little daughter, Minnie. The she-tiger in the Mrs. come out faster than a man will shoot if'n called a liar.

Soons Mrs. Fleck got back in town, and heard what happened, vengeance took over her brain. She went looking for the feller, but he danced away time and again. This morning, he got enticed in-to Mrs. Fleck's restaurant where a colored man throwed a lasso on him, and a bunch of us jumped the feller and tied him up. A colored feller lassoing a white man usually end up in a lynching, but hurting a child don't got no color. Mrs. Fleck took to whacking on this man with every implement she had at hand. Walloped him good and proper she did. My only regret is we didn't take the scoundrel to the river, tie a stone around his neck, and dump him in.

Downtown Garfield, Colorado, 1880
Donna Nevens Collection, Salida Regional Library, Salida, Colorado

July 23, 1883

Theys a bunch of arguing in town over that Presbyterian college. Some folks says it a money scam to get fellers to cough up cash with-out promise of no-thing. But the news-paper says there ain't no money due less'n the college come here for certain. Says lots of towns in the contest, and big cities, like Denver, already gots 2 or 3 such schools, and we need one. Says even Colorado Springs got a congregational college.

~

I seen 2 diagonal ditches, across F Street and G, but for the life of me I can't figure out what theys for. Don't no other fellers know either.

~

These new folks more aggravating than a boil on your butt during a long horse ride. Theys all bitching and moaning that the brothels are annoying the average citizen. Can't be annoying less'n you in ear-shot of the whores as they yell out from the windows, and that's only at night. I'm thinking it them new married ladies doing the complaining. I figure some of their husbands visiting the whore houses, on account of their wife ain't up to doing no poking lest she get with child. But good golly, sometimes a feller need relief. If'n a woman can't hold her man at home or have him keep his pecker in his pants she ought not ruin things for the rest of us. That just self-ish.

~

Them same folks upset the law on public obscenity ain't being enforced. If these fine folks ain't want to see a tit or hear a whore call out to suck a feller's prick they ought not be wandering the streets at night. What so damn hard about that?

~

Theys also busy bending ears over the numbers of loafers, bunko men, and pimps jamming the side-walks, yelling obscenities. I ain't gonna argue over the cussing, but what the hell they expect in a town with no-thing to do at nights except drink and gamble and fuck? Of course, them high and mighty types want the law to enforce the rule they set banning gambling tables, but that ain't gonna happen. Their new solution be to increase liquor license fees to bring in what they call 'higher class establishments.' Good God Almighty, there ain't enough rich fellers in town to support such. It just a sneaky way to bring in churches and dress shops and fancy restaurants so's working fellers like me get forced to move on down the line. Now that we done cleaned things up and built a proper town them damn money folk wanna take it all over. I'm madder than a buck during rut, I am.

THE VIRGINIA HOTEL.

Corner of First and F Streets.

NEW HOUSE. NEWLY FURNISHED. ROOMS COMMODIOUS AND PLEASANT. TABLE SUPPLIED WITH THE BEST. FIRST-CLASS IN EVERY RESPECT.

RATES $2 TO $3 PER DAY.

WAYSMAN BROS., Proprietors

Advertisement from The Salida Mail, 1883

CHAPTER EIGHT
August, 1883

August 2, 1883
    J.J. Gainey, employee of the rail-road, got arrested for pulling his revolver in Mix's Saloon. He came to town on his way to Denver to see his wife. They was a pay-check here for him, but the agent of the company ain't had the cash money to pay him so he had to stay in town to wait. He dropped into Mix's, took a drink, and was looking on at a stud-horse poker game. Mix were the dealer and asked Gainey to join him dollar for dollar. After he lost $3, Gainey quit. Mix offered to cash the check so's Gainey could keep going, and gave Gainey $15 in advance. Mix came back to the table after about 20 minutes and says only Gainey could cash the check. So's Gainey turned to go away at a loss when Mix says Gainey owed him $3. Gainey says he weren't to be robbed, and Mix punched him in the nose. Gainey drew his gun and told Mix to get behind the counter. Mix told the other players to let the feller leave with-out shooting him. 15 minutes later, Mix and a police officer found Gainey at the Gold Room Saloon. Gainey drew again, thinking Mix come to kill him when the officer announced he were the law. Gainey got took to jail. The law found govern-ment letters in Gainey's pockets, showing he weren't no thief. He still got fined for having a concealed weapon.

August 13, 1883
    Over to Canon City, a bunch of men called on Edward Watkins and says he got cattle what weren't his. He took the fellers to see the cows and they took a lot of 'em by force. Watkins brought suit, and says he can prove they his. Going to court in a few days.

~

Dr. Hallock's brother visiting from Iowa

~

Another fraternity, called Odd Fellows, planning a lodge in Salida.

~

We had a lot of visitors the last 2 weeks come in from back east. On vacation, they says. Can't say I ever had a vacation.

~

All the worker's at Arbour's Dance Hall got arrested. Theys plead guilt to running a house of prostitution and got fined $5 each. Ain't that some-thing? The whore houses get along just fine, but call your-self a dance girl, and folks get their noses bent.

~

I heard folks in Poncha joined the contest to get that Presbyterian College.

~

That violin player, Remenyi, one were here last year, coming back September 7. Time to save some coin. That feller could play.

August 14, 1883
Boys from Howard come to town to play our team in a game of base-ball. It weren't a contest. Salida boys won 55-2. Them Howard boys ain't played to-gether before, and it showed.

~

At the town council meeting, Pomeroy got named police judge. That mean the magistrate office open. Theys gave Stingley a pay raise to $90 a month.

~

Gillett and McGovern opened a new grocery on the east side of the alley on F Street.

~

D.E. Hanley opened a millinery, one door north of the Opera House.

~

W. Carpenter opened a watch-maker and jeweler opposite the post office.

August 18, 1883
Good God, Almighty, them folks in Canon City lost their minds. That Edward Watkins feller, one in jail waiting trial on cattle thieving, got took from the sheriff by a group of masked men around 1 in the morning. They dragged him to the old bridge crossing the river and hung him from the rail.

He had 18 cows what the law says belonged to others. Watkins told the judge he had papers showing he paid proper. Judge says they gonna hold Watkins over, and give him a chance to show the papers in court.

The sheriff took Watkins to his ranch out-side of Salida to get the papers. Theys went to his place, then took the mid-night train back, and was heading to the jail. It were mighty dark. A few steps from the court-house, theys met by 14-16 fellers in masks. Some grabbed the sheriff and held tight, told him he ain't getting hurt if'n he keep quiet.

Watkins took off running, and were met with a bunch of gun-shots over his head.

Later, after they cut his dead body down, the coroner found a fatal wound. Watkins got shot in the right breast, down-like, with the bullet stuck in his thigh. Most likely he were dead before he got hanged. That means he were on the ground when shot which a cowardly thing to do. Then theys hanged him which be double foul.

I ain't against a lynching when it be needed, but yanking a feller away from the law when a proper court trial under-way just in-tolerable.

August 20, 1883

Had a big meeting at the Opera House to express indignation at that Watkins lynching, and to pay respects to the murdered man. All the big whigs in town was there, and a good many ladies there too. It were civil, but folks mighty angry.

Judge Garrison called the meeting to order. Mr. McDevitt, Watkins lawy-yer, spoke and says the feller were a model citizen.

Reverend Hastings spoke, and says it were a deliberate, cold-blooded murder.

Judge Garrison talked, and says every-one know Mulock the biggest cattle thief in the county, and says he gonna put all his energies to finding the perpetrators of the dastardly act.

A few others had words, including Mr. North who says he seen Mulock and his men steal them cows from Watkins ranch.

August 21, 1883

Roller sold his furniture business to J. Witmaer and Company, who gonna keep running it a the same place on First Street. Roller spending his time with mining interests.

~

S.B. Westerfield opened his store with a bunch of notions, including collars, gloves, ribbons and boots.

~

Rail-road hired James J. O'Reilly to take care of the engines in the round-house. He knowed for being a solid worker who don't let the machines run hot, and keeps every-thing in order.

Commercial Hotel, Granite, Colorado, 1883
Patricia Bradbuy Holton Collection, Salida Regional Library, Salida, Colorado

CHAPTER NINE
September, 1883

September 2, 1883
That publisher feller came to town and gave me a big ole check for that book he printed with the first 2 years of journals. It were the most money I ever helt at one time.

I been mailing the journals to him regular, but ain't heard no-thing in near about a year. Figured I got took, but writing turns out to be a bit pleasure-able so I kept at it.

He says for me to buy some proper clothes, as this ain't no frontier village no more, but a real city. Says I should rent a house to boot and move out of my tent.

I ain't bought no suit, but I did get some new trousers, ones what ain't stained and odored from use, new long john's, and socks and boots with nary a hole. Tossed my ole hat too, which weren't easy as we been through a lot. Didn't get no fancy coat nor tie. Money ain't excite me enough to dress like a dude. I might of bought a few rounds, also.

~

I looked at some in-door living to-day. Rents on houses be high as the sky. Who the hell can pay such? Some-one gonna make a fortune if'n they build some small, neat homes what don't cost a arm and a leg. Think I'll stick to my tent for now. Burnt my old clothes as they were mighty odiferous. Even Sue had took to standing up-wind when we's to-gether. Ain't gonna shave my whiskers, but I did get a proper trim and a head washing. Felt down-right dainty doing such, but I look mighty pretty if'n I say so my-self, and I do.

~

I ain't the only one pissed off about the new liquor license fee of $600 theys discussing. Folks says it gonna slow down our growth, and I'm with 'em.

September 3, 1883
The cattle grower's convention were held in Poncha yester-day. I heard that talk got around to the Watkins lynching for cattle thieving. Seems theys a gang been working Chaffee County for some time, and they stoled over $200,000 of cattle. Says it started with only a hand-ful here and there, but as they ain't been caught nor punished, this gang now running off entire bunches, horses too. 60-70 head at a time.

July 6, Ernest Christison, local boy I wrote on, got his-self arrested up to South Park with 4 others. They changed some brands but were sloppy with it, and the old brands was easy to see.

And, it seems Watkins weren't the angel his law-yer made him to be, as some of them stole cows got their brands changed in his pasture, up above Salida

D.P. Fuller were their partner. He a feller what be super-intendent at the Calumet Mine.

They found these cattles at Watkins place not long ago. That's when them other fellers rode out to Watkins and took their cows back. But Watkins got some big balls and swore out a warrant on them boys, even tho they was content to let things be. That's when things turned sour.

When them cow-boys come to town for the law-suit Watkins filed, his gang, led by Mix, feller what own the worst gin-mill and gambling place in Salida, a place knowed for being a hang-out for thieves and gangs. Mix and a bunch of Watkins friends threatened to kill them ranchers, the ones answering the law-suit, first chance they had. But them ranchers played it cool, and ain't said a word. Stingley told 'em to head on out soon's their business were done, and that's what they did. Stingley friendly with that Watkins bunch, and drinks with 'em regular.

Them boys re-turned August 15 for the trial, but this time theys had 30 guns of their own, on account of they ain't seen where the law were gonna protect them in Salida. They weren't looking for no shooting, just protection. A bunch of 'em got off the train at Cleora and sent word ahead, so's theys no mis-understanding. The law says for them to stop at the Monte Cristo Hotel and they did the next morning. Theys had break-fast and stayed there until 2 in the after-noon when the trial were to happen. When theys went to court, they had a bunch of local ranchers protecting 'em plus the guns they brought.

The trial were held in the Opera House, and them cow-boys was all proper and respectful to every-one. They just ain't want to get shot at by Watkins gang. Theys stayed out of the saloons and laid low all around.

Well, you know the rest of the story as it went down in Canon City. Just goes to show the truth ain't no simple matter, and angels more oftener got horns holding up their halo.

September 6, 1883

Theys selling photo-graphs of James Bathurst, deputy what got murdered in May. Raising cash money for his wife and child who surely need it.

~

A.S. Hazaleus, experienced brick maker and mason, started a brick business 2 months ago, and already sold 60,000 of the 100,000 bricks he kilned. Most went to the building he working on for Haight and Churcher. Says he gonna burn 500,000 more by winter. These new buildings sure sturdier than the ones we had way back.

~

That publisher feller says I need to bathe at least weekly and not say 'fuck' nor 'shit' nor 'cocksucker' around ladies or society folks. Ain't that some-thing? I gots to admit the big check he brought speak louder than my pride, so's I figure watching my words a small thing to do. And a hot bath ain't half bad.

~

Speaking of society folk, they flocking here like geese. We done been found, that east coast man says. He says Salida now the place for money and society and business.

September 7, 1883

Mr. Green, city editor of *The Pueblo Chieftan*, passed through and wrote some beauty-ful words about Salida what I can't make better. So's, I cut it from the news-paper to paste in this journal.

September 8, 1883

Folks talking about putting to-gether what theys call a Building and Loan Association. Says such better suited to caring for citizens than would a bank.

~

I heard that last January, James Hughey, a fire-man for the rail-road, runned out on a bunch of bills in town. He left owing Mr. Carpenter $48, Byers and Myers, $28, Mrs. Bye $14, and $12 to the Ogden House. All these folks heard from some law-yers, Hughey and Atchison, that he were a scammer and they filed suit. Had his wages held, what they call garnishing, and to-day got some of the amount theys due, less'n what the law-yers took, of course.

September 9, 1883

Just before 2 in the morning, Mr. Whitney seen flames coming out of A.T. Ryan's livery stable. He told police-man Stewart who gave alarm by rapid firing his pistol. Nearly right away, 4 fire-men were on it.

The fire ate through all the wood and hay like it were no-thing, and spread all over. Jack Hogset took to the horses and got them out, but got his-self serious burnt. Johnny Burns saved 2 horses and Mr. Jackson, a rail-road employee, got to his team, tho 1 horse got burnt bad. Them fire-man had 3 power-ful streams on it, and soon it were under control, but all were lost for Ryan.

For a while, it look like the black-smith shop of J.J. Rockwell would catch, but it ain't.

September 12, 1883

Had a daring robbery at the home of Robert Patterson, what lives south-east of the school-house. His brother were visiting, asleep in another room, when some-one came in betwixt 8 at night and sun-rise. Stole the brothers pocket-book, what had $131 cash, a heavy silver watch, and some rail-road passes. The pants was set on the head of the bed and the watch were dis-connected from a chain. Either this boy is telling a big one or theys a feller in town what don't know fear.

~

Salida sure gots some big-hearted peoples. J.W. Williams led the charge, and folks and businesses donated $1,200 to help A.T. Ryan re-start his livery business as'n he ain't had no insurance.

~

I swear, were it not for the big check that publishing feller brought I'd soon skipped this one, but I went to hear a lady name Nellie E. Ellsworth do what they call a reading. And that's what it be—a lady reading out loud. It were at the Opera House, and those what went called it 'excellent.' I calls it mildly tolerable, but it ain't held water to fiddle playing nor a good story-telling. The news-paper feller says her diction were perfect, which I took to mean she ain't a mumbler, her impersonations accurate, and her acting dramatic. What were dramatic were the speed I showed getting out of there after it were done.

~

Group of locals met with the Baptist mission, at the Presbyterian Church, and decided to open a congregation in Salida. Yet another church. Law-yers and churches, churches, and law-yers. Weren't long ago it were blood, booze, and whores, but such things seem long ago.

~

Reverend Hastings did some some preaching Sunday at the Opera House. Reverend McDade did the same over to the Methodist church.

September 13, 1883

The county hospital gots 13 rail workers in it and 5 locals. Theys all full up.

~

E.S. Armstrong, feller holding rights to the Duryee process in Chaffee County, talking of putting a smelter here what can handle 100 tons of ore a day.

~

The little boy of Mr. Downing got dog bit, but it weren't serious. Been my boy, I'd be biting on a dog, and that's a fact.

~

The little boy of Mr. Miller, what been dangerously ill with the typhoid, up and out again.

~

Johnson and Chenoweth contracted with Edward Corbin, grocery feller, to build him a 2-story house, 7 room Mansard roof
home. Sounds mighty fancy.

~

A thief tried to break in to Mrs. Collins restaurant, the one over on First Street. She were sleeping up-stairs. The first try, she thought it were her son coming home late. The second try, she got up, and must of scared the thief as he run off.

September 15, 1883

Guess I ain't gots to be too worried about Salida getting duded up just yet.

Yester-day morning, 2 well-known cow-boys, name Frank Reed and Bent Jamison, came to town armed to the teeth and parading it for all to see, up and down the streets.

Marshal Stingley were cool as a water-melon. He politely in-formed them fellers about the ordinance against carrying weapons in the city limits and asked them to lay their guns aside. They said they would.

Around 12 noon, they went toward the stable, the one in the rear of Mrs. Fleck's restaurant, to get their horses and leave town. By this time, a warrant were put in-to the Marshal's hands. It were from the sheriff of Saguanche County and were for Bent Jamison who were under indictment there. Stingley grabbed up his deputy, Mr. Frizelle, and rushed over before them cow-boys could ride out. Reed were already mounted, but Jamison were standing in the lot, near the stable door.

"Bent," the Marshal says, "I have a warrant for you." Stingley's hands was in the pockets of his hunting coat—one pocket had the warrant, the other a small pistol.

"I'll never be taken alive," Jamison says and draws a .45.

I was watching, and you could see Stingley twitch as he thought to shoot the feller. Weren't Stingley's first round-up facing a gun, and I reckon he ain't liked the idea of being slow to draw again. I seen Stingley look over his shoulder. He seen Reed with a Winchester, cocked and leveled at Stingley and Frizelle. One of them were gonna die for sure. Stingley a cool one, tho. He kept talking and walking slow toward Jamison, backing him to the door. But there weren't no edge to be had, so's Stingley left, run down the street for a shot-gun and some help. But them cow-boys was fast. Theys long gone time the Marshal re-turned.

~

Theys more cattle vanishing in Chaffee and Fremont county. Mr. Amy from Howard Creek lost 10 head last week and JH. Freeman lost 5 or 6 calves. Law gonna have to get serious or theys be some serious blood spilt. Them cattle fellers says enough be enough.

September 18, 1883

Town council met last night and read the re-signation of Marshal Baxter Stingley. He thought it fair to step down as'n he running for county sheriff next month. The council says no, it fair he stay on the job here as marshal. Says he can re-sign if'n he gets elected.

~

J.S. Painter filed charges for Jacob Strossheim against deputy marshal Stewart for what he calls conduct un-becoming a officer. Guess that means he were in-tolerable rude.

~

Things around the rail-road shops getting busier and busier. Gonna have 37 machines when the latest building done.

~

Dang if our streets ain't a thing to see. Never seen 'em look better. Clean and level and proper.

~

The Salida Hose Company wrote a letter in the paper asking the town for help. Says they ain't near enough hose to reach fires and that theys all tired of losing a suit of clothes every-time they fights a fire. Asking for rubber over-coats to protect what they got on, and for proper head-gear so's they don't get whacked by falling timbers and such.

September 19, 1883

Grand jury found 5 indictments against Thomas Ninemeyer. One for intent to kill Marshal Stingley, one for murder of Deputy Bathurst, one for murder of Mr. Brown, one for causing murder of Evans, and one for murder of Mr. Gannon. Cock-sucker says he not guilty to all. Trial coming in a few days.

~

Society of the Methodist Episcopal church, organized not long ago, gonna start building in a few days. Church will be 40 feet by 60. The Baptists and the Catholics also talking about building in Salida. Did I says it or did I not? We about to be hip deep in tea-totalers and law-suits. Lord, help us.

~

General William Tecumsah Sherman his-self pulled up at the depot this morning. A news-paper feller run up on him and the general were a little suspicious. Their conver-sation were down-right hilarious, as'n the General weren't up for talking.

"General, is this trip of yours one of business or pleasure?" says the reporter.

"Young man, it is a combination of both," says Sherman.

"General, how long do you expect to be gone from home on this trip?"

"Till I get back."

"You are on your way to Salt Lake, are you not?"

"Yes sir, I am. By the way, young man, it seems to me you are getting too cute. If I tell you all I know you will know as much as I do. Good day."

They was more said, but thems the funny parts.

Methodist Episcopal Church, 1883
Haley-Braton Collection, Salida Regional Library, Salida, Colorado

September 23, 1883

Lots being said around town about that high liquor license fee theys proposing. Those for it says the higher fee will close the second-rate places. Them be the ones working fellers go to, like me and the rail-road men. They says first-rate joints can do well enough and it's them theys wanting in Salida going forward. They says the other saloons ain't no-thing but dead-fall, and sooner they get pushed out of town the better. They says them places sell rot gut what makes a feller violent and a thief.

Ain't none of us stupid. What they says in low-voice conversation is Salida ain't looking dainty enough for the money men, fellers they call capitalists, to be impressed and feeling safe when they comes here to buy the land and make businesses.

This all about no-thing but money, and any son of a whore what says different a damn liar.

I knowed this was coming. Said so from the get-go.

~

Baxter Stingley officially running for sheriff of Chaffee County. Don't think he gots a chance, cuz the money fellers ain't backing him. He shaking hands and asking for votes, but I ain't seen no feller win no-thing what ain't had the money behind 'em, and he don't.

~

I knowed I shouldn't have, but I damn near busted a gut laughing at a meeting last night over to the Opera House. Folks looked at me like I passed gas in church. What were it made me loose my manners? Theys organizing to build a gymnasium. What that be? A place for folks to do what they calls exercise. That's what money folk need cuz they don't do no proper work, getting their hands dirty and shirts sweaty. Ain't that some-thing? Theys even elected officers. Ben DeRemer, president; E.E. Williams, vice president; Dr. O'Connor, secretary; Frank Crozer, treasurer. Gonna charge folks $5 a month, a month I says, to be a member. That on top of $2 just to get the right to pay $5 a month. Already got 50 folks signed up. I shit you not.

September 25, 1883

The doctors in town all complaining cuz don't no-one get sick around here.

~

Theys a push from some merchants to close all the stores on Sunday. Says it ain't civilized to do business on the Sabbath.

~

I dang near wet my trousers laughing to-day. Stranger walked in-to Judge Bowne's, on the corner by Pomeroy's office, and asked where the Presbyterian church were. Judge scratched his head. It were obvious he ain't knowed. He turned to Jack Williams and asked him. Jack says he ain't knowed either. I ain't questioning the morals of either fellers, but even a drunk like me knows where the only church in town located.

~

This morning, Charles Ferritt filed a complaint against John Long, says Long stole $15 from him. Officer Stewart arrested Ferritt and, sure enough, found the cash on his person. Justice Pomeroy fined Ferrit $25 plus costs, and tossed him in the cooler until he pays. That ain't what you call a profitable transaction.

~

I do like the rail workers. Them boys know how to throw a proper shin-dig. Put it to-gether fast, too.

A tele-graph came yester-day saying loco-motive fire-men from back east would arrive in the evening, passing through on a trip. The boys got to hopping, arranging with hotels for rooms and the Opera House for a ball.

About 10:45 at night, the train roll in with 300 fire-men, some who had wives or sweethearts, filling every dang hotel in town. Theys all had a hearty supper then went over to the Opera House where the ball were already swinging. They were some speeching, of course, by some lodge leaders. Then there was dancing, and a bunch of it, until near mid-night.

Next morning, they got took to Marshall Pass then back here for dinner. Fellers were extra polite, apologizing for no advance notice. A right proper bunch of men they was.

"Reaching Salida as the sun went down, it seemed to us we had never seen so pretty a town anywhere. It is all so clean, so neat and attractive. Through it flows the rapid Arkansas, free here from stagnant bars or swampy banks. On its east bank are the pretty new stone passenger depot of the Denver & Rio Grande railway, the big new stone round house of the same road, and the handsome Monte Christo hotel, at the foot of a bold bluff fringed with pines. Crossing the river, on a temporary bridge replacing one recently washed away by the freshet, we find ourselves immediately in the town of Salida. It is not at all built on one street, like most of our western towns, but is well built out, and begins to take the shape of a thriving young city. The buildings all have a new and attractive appearance, well suited to the unrivaled location of the town. The valley here is from two to six miles wide.

CHAPTER TEN
October, 1883

October 1, 1883
I'm thinking Salida need to organize a dude club. Ain't never seen so many fellers, all new to town, with their hair parted straight down the middle and slicked back. What use-less specimens of humanity. They ain't of western origin, I guarandamntee, but have strayed from the east.

~

Theys a woman going around Maysville saying she Mrs. Bathurst, widow of the deputy, murdered here in Salida. She asking for for cash money to help her get by. It ain't Mrs. Bathurst tho. She were horry-fied to hear such. Shameful.

~

The Salida Cornet Band got new instruments the other evening at Dickman's. Them boys surprised their leader, Frank W. Wood, with a magnificent cornet of his own. Shocked he were. He brought out a box of cigars to celebrate.

~

Last night, about 1 in the morning, Mr. Carpenter, who sleeps in his store, got woke by some-one trying to get in the front door. Feller were putting a knee on the door and pushing and pulling the knob. Carpenter watched a minute from in-side, then spoke to the man, who took to his heels and made a escape. Carpenter says it good for the feller he ain't got in-side, cuz he would've heard music in the air which were interesting to all but the person most concerned.

October 9, 1883
If building any indication, then Salida be prospering.

~

Ths morning, around 9, we all heard a terrible explosion in the direction of the planning mill. Weren't long until a crowd streamed that way. The worst fears was true. The boiler exploded and instantly killed J.H. Moody, the proprietor, feller what owns the lumber yard. He were working at the planer, nearly in front of the boiler, sharpening knives with a file. The force threw him 40 feet in-to the yard, next to a pile of lumber.

~

Machinery been coming for the rail-road shops. Theys one 7-foot planer, lathes of different sizes, 2 drill presses, 1 bolt cutter, 1 pipe cutter. All running smooth as a watch. Them boys sure proud of their new tools.

~

Senator Hill were greeted at the Opera House last night by one of the biggest audiences I ever seen in Salida. He came to talk about what happening in Congress with silver and tariffs, big news here. He got a rousing reception. We a city for sure when big whigs come calling.

October 12, 1883
Ryan opened his new livery stable.

~

Members of the Methodist Episcopal church met to organize a Sabbath school. 13 folks there, 4 was childrens.

~

It official. The town board raised the fees for saloons to $600 a year. Tried to be sneaky. It $200 a year for a saloon fee, $400 for the liquor license. I ain't great at cyphering, but that still $600. Church folk and money men won again.

~

That Presbyterian college going to Del Norte.

October 27, 1883
25 big whig business fellers from Denver came through last night after a hunting trip through the San Luis valley. Had 1,000 rabbits. Says they'd got more if'n not for running out of ammunition. When they left Denver, they had 8 half-barrels and
9 quarter barrels of beer. Finished the last of it here in Salida.

October 28, 1883
Lord a mighty, Lord a mighty, what terrible sad times. I shed my tears along with others. Marshal Baxter Stingley got shot down in cold blood. He dead.

Remember way back to the Lake County War days, and not so long ago to the cattle thief what were lynched? And that night Frank Reed backed Stingley off serving a warrant? All them birds come home to roost to-day.

Frank Reed done the murder. He part of that cattle-thieving bunch, with Edward Watkins and Ernest Christison and others. When not a thief he worked in Mix and Company's brick-yard. Ain't no one what weren't aware them boys stoled cows. Only no-one done no-thing about it, and now the Marshal be dead.

Reed bragged he won't never get taken alive for his crimes, and seems his word true as'n he gone from town, and Stingley's dead.

At 8:30 to-night, Stingley went in-to Arbour's Variety and Dance Hall. Stingley seen a writer for the news-paper and had a few words. Stingley then seen Reed and turned right, and walked straight up to the man cuz Reed gots a warrant for his arrest. Reed were talking to a bar-keep.

Stingley always had 2 guns, fine ones. He carried 1 with a bull-dog pattern, ivory handle and blue steel barrel. The other were a Colt .45, silver-plated. Stingley pulled the bull-dog one with his left hand, and spoke to Reed. I gonna remember them words the rest of my days.

"Frank, I have a warrant for you, throw up your hands."

Them boys knowed one another through Edward Watkins, lynched feller who were a firm friend of Stingley. Lots of folks ain't knowed they shared a house at one point. Watkins and Stingley was so close that when Stingley heard of the lynching, he headed straight back from Texas, where he were on a business matter, and swore vengeance. I don't know if Reed were one of those Stingley had in mind.

Usually a sound thinker, Stingley, showed poor judgment in the matter with Reed. Instead of standing a few feet off, with Reed covered by his gun, Stingley put the barrel of the gun against Reed's side. If'n he'd shoved the muzzle in-to Reed's ribs, he mighta been good. But he weren't. Remember it were only last month when

Reed got the advantage on Stingley, forcing him to back down, and my thinking is that stuck in his craw, hurting is pride.

Frank were standing with his hands in his coat pocket. He yanked his hands out of his pockets and, quick as lightning, grabbed Stingley's gun away, covering the Marshal with his own weapon. They stared a few seconds, then Stingley went for his other gun, and Reed fired. He fired again and Stingley fired back. Reed then took off for the door, turned, and fired once more as Stingley chased after.

When Reed run out the door, the Marshal stopped, which weren't like him. I got sick to my stomach cuz I knowed ain't but one thing make a man like Baxter Stingley give up the chase. He were shot bad.

Mr. Arbour and that news-paper feller called out, asking if he were shot.

"Yes," Stingley said, his legs all wobbly. "He shot me 3 times."

A bunch of us, and Mr. Arbour, grabbed Stingley and laid him out on a table. We took off his boots for comfort, and both was filled up with blood. A god-awful mess it were. Mr. Arbour says to move the Marshal to a private room and we done just that.

Dr. Underhill were there by then and he took over. The Marshal had 3 separate gun-shot wounds. 1 were through the right thigh. 1 were through the left arm. The last 1 were about 2 inches below his left nipple. Doc says Stingley got shot in what they call a artery, some-thing what carry all the blood, and he were done for. The Marshal ain't had a chance to survive.

He were only 38-years-old.

~

His proper name were Benjamin Baxter Stingley. Born 1845 in Iowa, where he gots a father. His brother, Jessie, what lived here a while, headed out for the Washington Territory. Baxter got a married sister and a uncle over in Missouri. He ain't never married nor had childrens.

Stingley came out this way 18 years ago, doing a little of every-thing, including mining and bar-keeping. He were marshal of Salida 2 years. First one to last longer than a few months. He were loved and respected by all, and never one to shirk his duties. Every-one wanted him as sheriff of the county, but out-side money beat him. They ain't gonna find a braver man to take over.

Benjamim 'Baxter' Stingley, 1845-1883

CHAPTER ELEVEN
November, 1883

Noember 1, 1883
　I listened in on some bad fellers saying Frank Reed were paid that cattle-thieving gang to kill Marshal Stingley. Says it were no accident. I don't know about such but wouldn't surprise me none.
　～
　Ernest Christison in jail over to Buena Vista for his own safety. Sheriff Painter grabbed him first thing the morning after the murder and held him under guard until the transport.

November 2, 1883
　Town council offering $1,000 cash money reward for the capture of Frank Reed. Theys also asked Colorado Governor Grant to pitch in another $1,000.

November 3, 1883
　They laid Baxter Stingley to rest to-day. All the flags at half-mast. All the businesses closed.
　Every train coming in-to the city last night brought family and friends to attend the sad last rites. At a early hour this morning, the streets were crowded to attend the funeral.
　Knights of Pythias did the funeral. They formed in front of their hall and marched to the under-taker to escort the body to the Opera House. They was joined by the band and the fire company.
　They all marched in-side at 11, and the place ain't had no room left.
　Reverend A.B. Fields preached. He talked about Stingley's bravery doing his duty, of his honor, that he never shrank from danger. He said words about the loss to Stingley's family. He said true words, that Stingley won't ever be for-got in the history of Salida.
　Every-one took up the offer to view the remains, and that took quite a while. Seems the entire Valley, and a good part of the rest of the country, showed up. It were the largest funeral ever held in this county. Over 3,000 folks.
　Then, they formed a parade to march to Cleora to bury Stingley in the cemetery. In order, they lined up with the marshal of the day, the hearse, the Knights of Pythias, all in uniform, the fire company, and officers of the city. The rest of us followed, some in carriages, some on horse-back or foot.
　When we got to the cemetery, the band played Baxter's favorite tune. Weren't one of us not shedding tears. The preacher said a few words, then they lowered the body in-to the ground. The Knights of Pythias and

the fire company surrounded the grave, and they went through a impressive ceremony.

November 6, 1883
This here was printed directly from the Colorado Governor: *It being represented to me that Baxter Stingley, the marshal of the town of Salida, and a deputy sheriff of Chaffee county, was, on the night of the 28th of October, 1883, murdered by one Frank Reed: and, WHEREAS, It is represented that said Frank Reed is a noted outlaw and desperado, and that said murder was committed in a felonious and premeditated manner, while the said Baxter Stingley was in the discharge of his duty, in making the arrest of said Frank Reed; and, WHEREAS, Said Reed has escaped, and successfully eludes the officers of said county in effecting his arrest and capture, and, WHEREAS, the mayor of Salida has offered a reward of $1,000 for his arrest; and, WHEREAS, I am petitioned by a large number of the citizens of said county to offer an additional reward of $1,000, now, Therefore, I, James B. Grant, governor of the state of Colorado, do hereby offer a reward of $1,000 for the arrest and delivery of the said Reed to the proper authorities of said county of Chaffee.*
JAMES B. GRANT, Governor

November 16, 1883
The Salida Hose Company threatening to dis-band. Theys only got 60 feet of hose in fit condition and ain't got proper gear to wear.

~

Looks like Salida taking in all the other towns. Lots of businesses moving here. Most recent, Mr. Peck of Vicksburg opened a saloon in Judge Bowne's buildings and M. Coleman of Bonanza started moving his stock of queens-ware to a room under the Opera House.

~

Mr. Arbour building on to his dance hall. Adding a 16 by 90 foot addition to start a variety theater.

November 23, 1883
Salida gots at least 1,000 more folks than Buena Vista, yet that little village still says they ought to stay the county seat. It seem they blind to truth. That place going down-hill. Won't matter. 1 year from to-day, it will be no-thing but a little hood-lum town with no-thing more than a court house tax-payers paid for.

~

Now that I gots new threads and took to bathing once a week, doctors and society folk ain't so reluctant to have a sit-down talk. They says we gots about 400 children here, half not old enough for school. But in the last 18 months, only 3 died from natural causes. And only 3 adults died that way. They says that don't happen no-where else. Theys don't know if it be the altitude or the lack of moisture but says this valley be a natural sanitarium, which mean place what don't got lots of germs. I'm hoping all my new-found bathing ain't taking away my natural pro-tections from such. I ain't got proper ill far back as I re-call.

~

Dude from back east showed me a news-paper today. What they calls the *New York Times* gots a article on the murder of Baxter Stingley.

IN MEMORIAM.

WHEREAS, It has pleased the Divine Ruler of the Universe to remove from our midst while at his post of duty, our dearly beloved brother, Baxter Stingley, thereby causing us to mourn the loss of one who, as a member of this lodge has always been true and faithful in the discharge of his duties, and whose daily life and walk was a living example of the true knight, always brave in defending the right, and equally courageous in prosecuting the wrong, and

WHEREAS, by the untimely death of Brother Stingley this lodge has met with irreparable loss, he being one of its most earnest and faithful members; Salida and Chaffee county, one of its most useful citizens, and humanity one of its noblest defenders, yet we humbly bow to the mandates of him who doeth all things well, and hope that what is our loss will be His gain.

CHAPTER TWELVE
December, 1883

December 5, 1883
About 4 this morning, Mr. North were bringing the east mail to the post office. He got met by a rough-looking character wanting to know what were in the wheel-barrow. North said it ain't none of his business. The feller ask if'n he carrying registered packages, and North says it be dangerous if'n the feller tries to find out. The man kept following, but he heard some-one coming and lit out.

~

Gillett and McGovern had their store robbed by a couple of burglars. They bore out a part of the door sash, and reached in and turned the lock. Thieves pried off the money draw and took $2-$3 in change, all that were left. Also took a can of peaches and a can of milk. Them thieves also broke in-to Slater's black-smith shop and stole a brace and a bit, which they used on the grocery. It were snowing at the time, so's their tracks easy to see. Theys took off over a fence.

December 15, 1883
At 12 noon to-day, a cutting fray took place in the DandRG yard betwixt Robert Scott and James Brady. Seems Brady, Scott, and a man name Lampson came here last year from Gunnison. Whilst they was hanging to-gether, Lampson lost $60. To-day, Scott says Brady stole the money, and they started fighting. Brady cut off a chunk of Scott's ear. Scott stabbed Brady about 4 inches
deep. Dr. O'Connor fixed both boys up. Scott got fined $20. He ain't had no money, so he now in jail.

December 20, 1883
Traveler wrote to the news-paper about what they seen in Salida It were full of flowery words about humming business and the $40,000 a month the rail-road pays to local workers. What made me near fall off my chair with sickn-ess were the words about Arbour's Dance Hall.

"It is large and being made larger by the old sinner who runs it. Here were about 100 cow-boys and miners in their glory—drinking, smoking, gambling and dancing. About 20 painted pullets swing in the giddy dances and kick as high and drink as deep as their rugged partners. There are several blood stains on the floor, and 1 large blotch were made by the life currents of Marshal Stingley a few weeks ago. But this roughness is overbalanced by the onward of education and social refinement, and Salida will yet be as good as she is pretty."

December 21, 1883
    City council met last night to take up the bridge question. J.C. Paterson got the contract cuz he were low bidder. Theys to be 2 stone piers built, 1 at each end of the river. Says it be done by April.

~

    The Masonic lodge up and running, Salida Lodge of A.F. and A.M., meaning Ancient Free and Accepted Mason. Had a feast to celebrate with lots of speeching.

December 23, 1883
    Some folk stupid-er than a tender-foot on the trail.
    They was a court trial of a robber, who entered Pender and Wyman's store. The lawy-er what prosecuting ask the thief if'n he employed a attorney. The feller ain't under-stood, so's the law-yer ask again if he employed a attorney. The thief just look at him dumb-like, then says, "No, thank you. I have no use for a tool of that kind."

1883 INSURANCE MAPS OF SALIDA

*Sanborn Fire Insurance Map from Salida, Chaffee County, Colorado
Sanborn Map Company, Sep, 1886*

FRONT

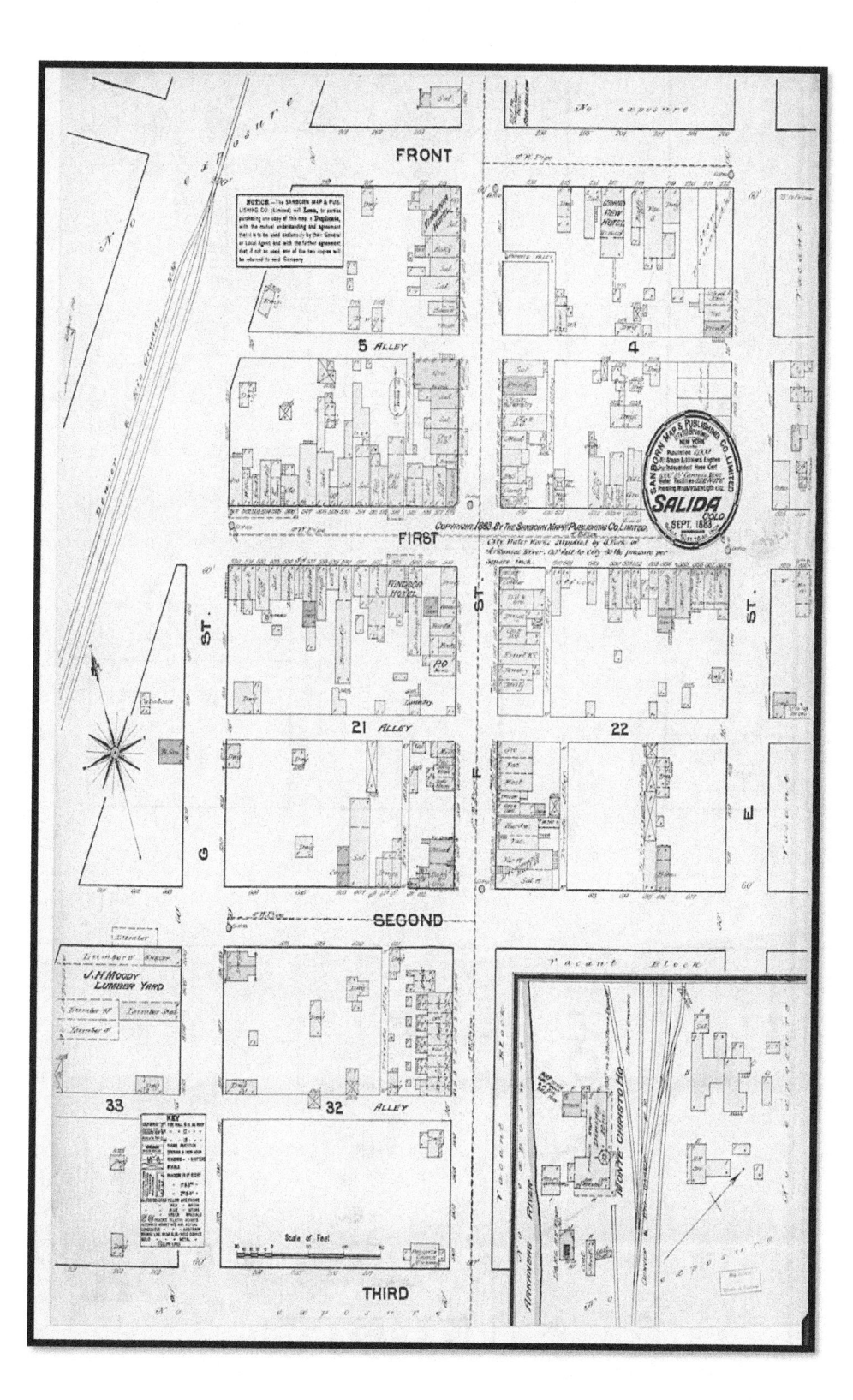

SALIDA
COLO.
SEPT. 1883

FIRST ST.

SECOND

THIRD

No exposure

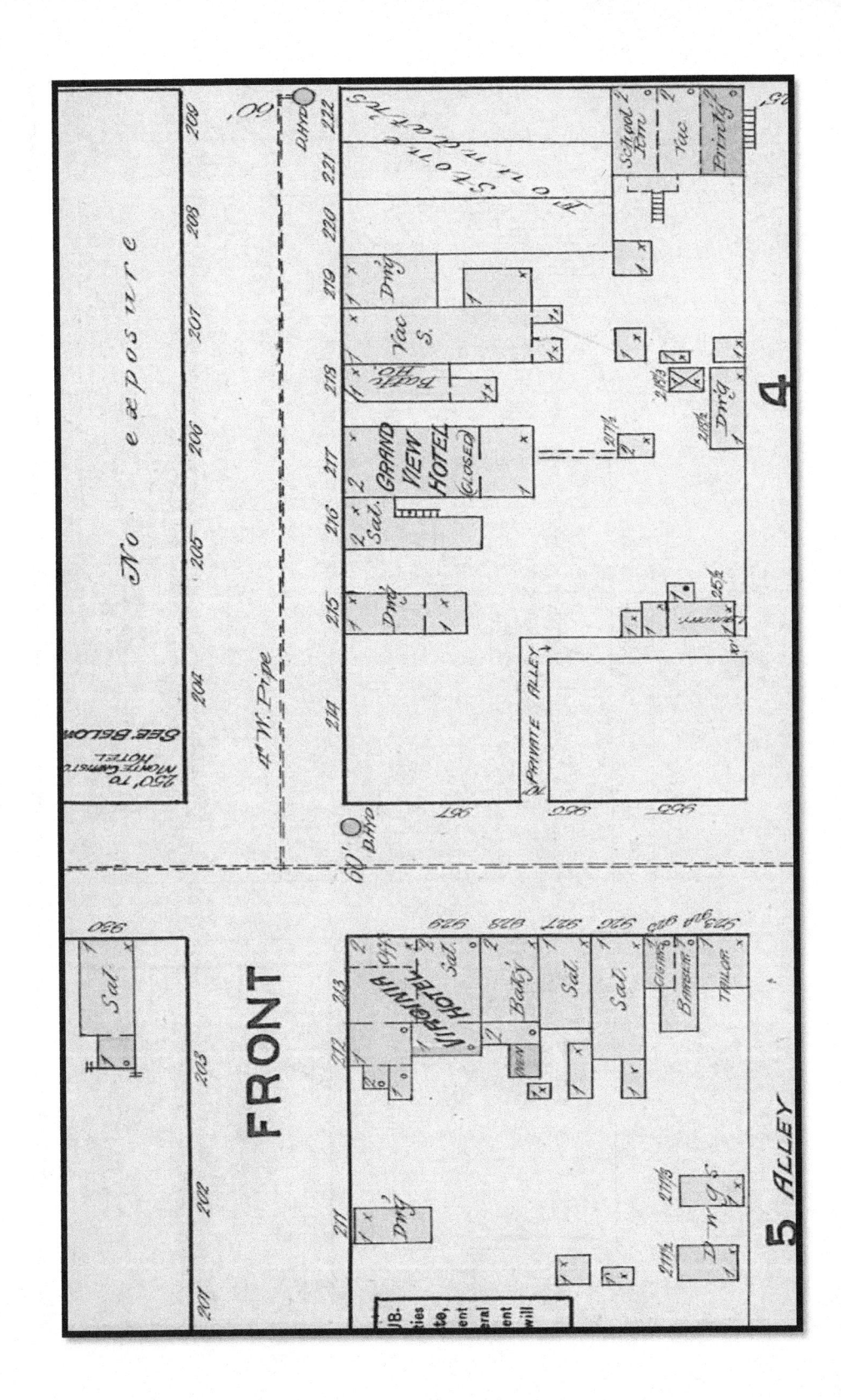

FRONT

5 Alley

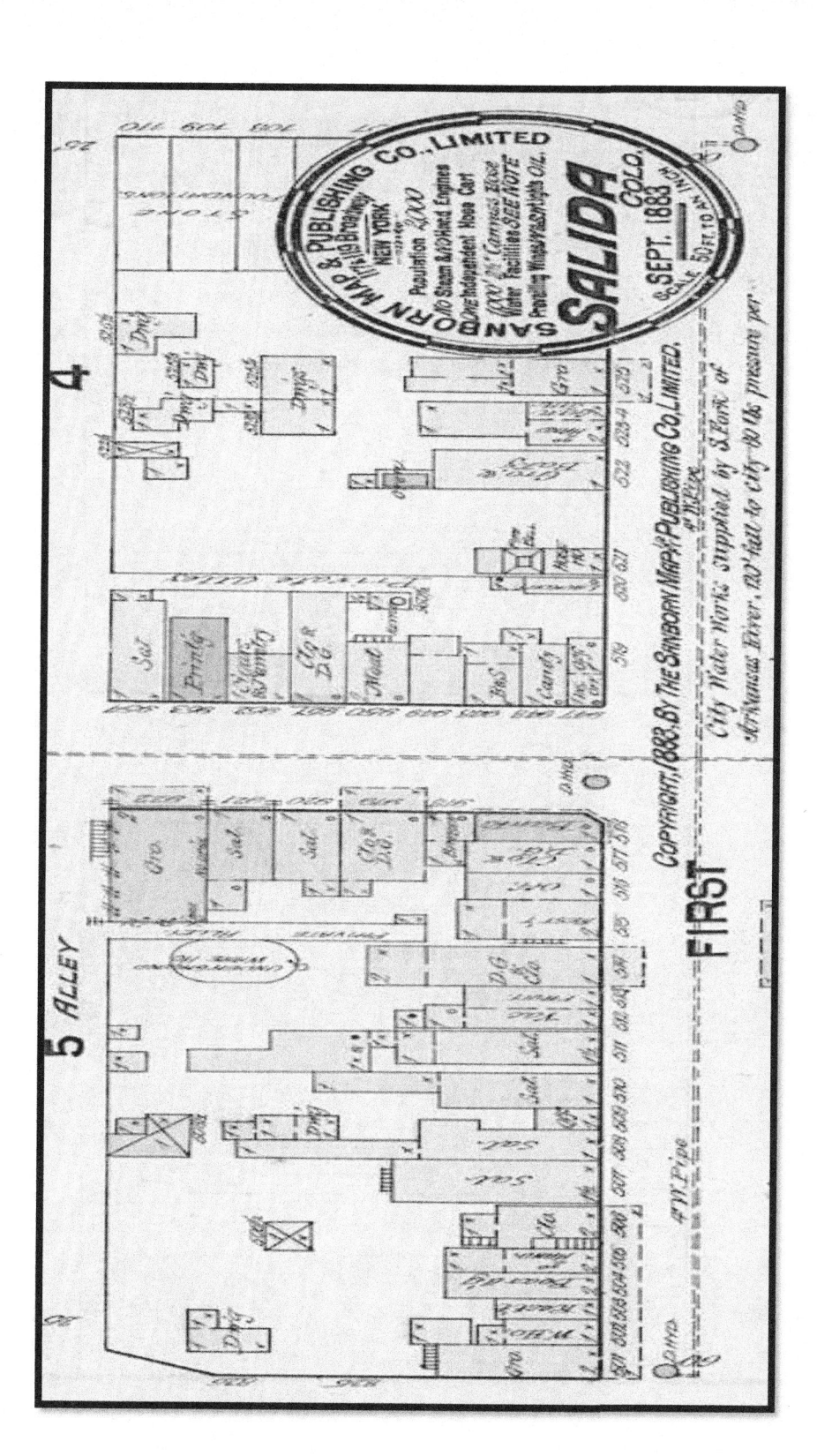

SANBORN MAP & PUBLISHING CO., LIMITED
117 & 119 Broadway, NEW YORK

SALIDA, COLO.
SEPT. 1883
SCALE 50 FT. TO AN INCH

Population 2000
Steam & % Head Engines
One Independent Hose Cart
Water Facilities SEE NOTE
Prevailing Winds S.W. to S.E. Oct. to April

COPYRIGHT, 1883, BY THE SANBORN MAP & PUBLISHING CO., LIMITED.

City Water Works supplied by S. Fork of Arkansas River. 120' fall to city. 80 lbs pressure per 4" Pipe.

FIRST

City Water Works supplied by S. Fork of Arkansas River. 120 ft fall to city–80 lbs pressure per square inch.

ARKANSAS RIVER

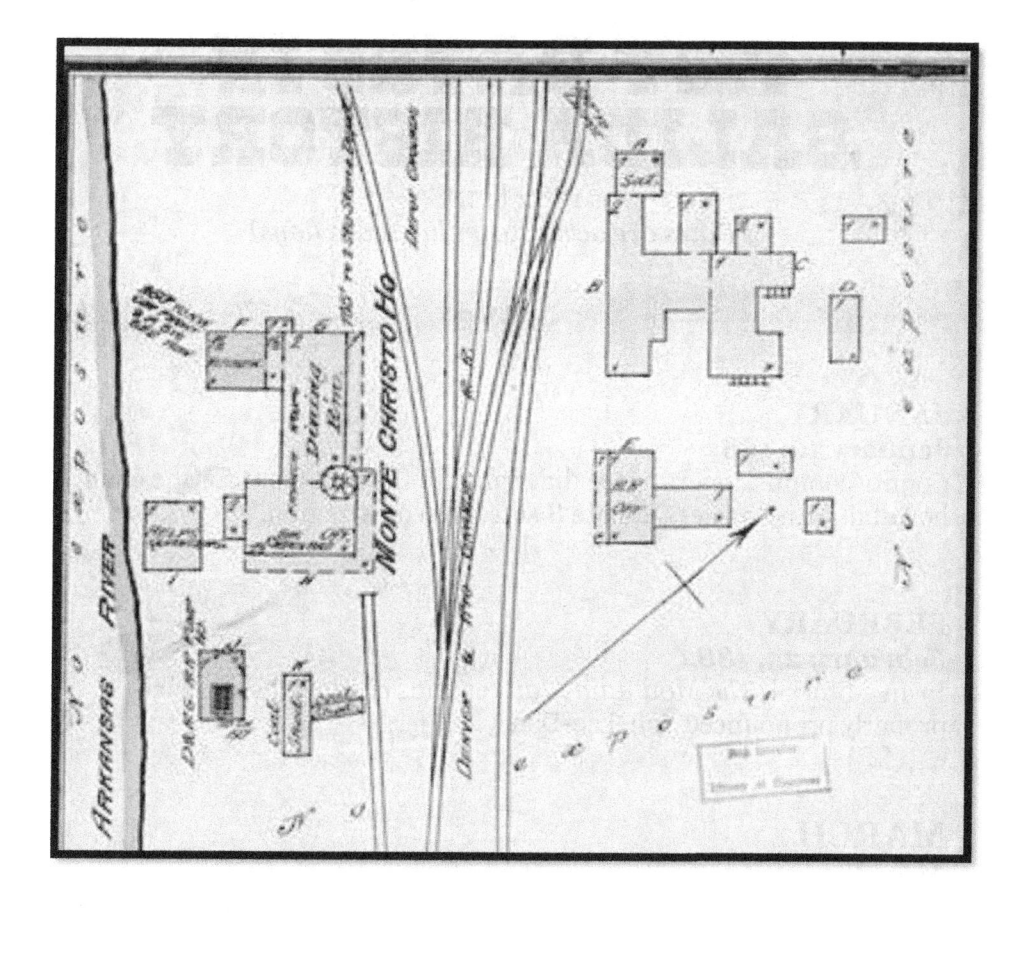

MONTE CHRISTO Ho.

Denver & Rio Grande R.R.

KEY DATES IN SALIDA HISTORY

1882 & 1883
(Dates are accurate within seven days)

1882

JANUARY
January 10, 1882
County commissioners agree that Salida is the best place for the county hospital. Land owners donate 8 acres for construction.

~

FEBRUARY
February 25, 1882
In an editorial, *The Mountain Mail* reminds citizens their town is properly pronounced Sah-Lee-Dah.

MARCH
March 7, 1882
Busines begin a mass migration from First Street to the north end of F Street to be closer to the railroad depot.

March 12, 1882
An editorial bemoans the high rents of homes and asks why no one constructs smaller, affordable homes.

March 14, 1882
When Olney retires, he and Moore dis-solved their partnership of *The Mountain Mail*.

March 30, 1882
The hills between the roundhouse and machine shop are now jammed with shanty houses.

APRIL
April 3, 1882
A new addition to Salida is laid out on the south-east edge of town, the project of Blake, Hodgman, and Westerfield. The new area has streets in line with compass directions rather than the river.

April 28, 1882
Lamp posts are placed at the foot of F Street bridge.

MAY
May 12, 1882
Night lights are placed along Front Street, in front of Hawkins Hotel and Wilson's Grocery.

JUNE
June 3, 1882
Knight of Pythias organize. Their lodge is named Iron Mountain Lodge number 19.

June 4, 1882
Denver and Rio Grande is ranted a right-of-way on Fourth Street and I to put in tracks.

JULY
July 10, 1882
Webb and Corbin begin construction of their new brick building, on the corner of F Street and the alley.

July 17, 1882
A small group of Italians come to town to work on the round-house.

AUGUST
August 8, 1882
Strayer's addition to town completed a survey, northwest of town. 25 acres north-west of town with 10 blocks and 22 lots.

SEPTEMBER
September 26, 1882
Bank of Salida officially fails. Their assets are turned over to the newly formed Chaffee County Bank. The owner of this bank started the original Chaffee County Bank, but sold it a year prior.

1883

FEBRUARY
February 27, 1883
Salida's population tops 3,000. There are now 100 businesses in town, including eighteen saloons, one bank, five hotels, nine groceries, three meat markets, three hardware stores, four hardware stores, three bakeries, and six restaurants.

MAY
May 3, 1883
The new railroad hotel, built beside the depot, is named the Monte Cristo.

May 5, 1883
The city of Salida plants trees along Front Street (now Sackett Avenue), from E Street to G Street.

May 30, 1883
Deputy Marshal James Bathurst, two citizens, Mr. Gannon and William Brown, and an outlaw, Tom Evans are murdered in a shootout with Thomas Ninemeyer and his gang. Marshal Baxter Stingly is seriously wounded, but survives.

JUNE
June 4, 1883
The Mountain Mail is renamed *The Salida Mail*.

AUGUST
August 13, 1883
Edward Watkins is lynched in Canon City after being accused of cattle theft.

SEPTEMBER
September 12, 1883
Baptist and Catholic congregations meet to plan churches.

September 15, 1883
Frank Reed and Bent Jamison back down Marshal Baxter Stingley and his deputy. As the Marshal attempted to serve a warrant on Jamison, Reed drew a rifle and forced the retreat.

September 19, 1883
The Methodist Episcopal church being construction of their new building on the corner of D Street and Fourth Street.

September 23, 1883
A group of locals form an organization to construct a gymnasium.

OCTOBER
October 28, 1883
Marshal Baxter Stingley is murdered by Frank Reed while attempting to serve a warrant.

CHRONOLOGY OF KEY SALIDA CITIZENS

1882 & 1883
(Dates are accurate within seven days)

George F. Bateman

June 16, 1880
Got another new business looking to give this Mulvany feller a run for his money. G.F. Bateman gonna also sell hard-ware and tin-ware on First Street near G. Cant see both making it.

April 8, 1881
Our elections, such as they was, got W.A. Hawkins for mayor over Blake 50-48. French, Bateman, Craig, and Wilson trustees.

June 18, 1881
Bender roofed his new building in tin and Bateman supervised.

July 28, 1881
Town folk having a big ole meeting over at Hunt's building to talk about pushing Salida as home for the State capital. Judge Hawkins gonna to be there, along with the Craig brothers, Blake, French, Bateman, Smith, Devereux, Hartzell, Howell, Webb and Corbin, Israel, Galbraith, the Wilsons, Roller, Twitchell, and a few others.

March 19, 1882
Theys asked, but Mr. Bateman don't want to be a town trustee no more. Says he too busy. Smart feller what don't wade deep in-to politics. Wish more fellers was so bright.

April 9, 1882
Bateman following the others and putting a new front on his store to face F Street along with Hively and Young. F Street the official main street it seems. First and Second less import-ant every day.

June 3, 1882
With all the sick-ness in town, Salida paid George Bateman to build a pest house. Cost $20.

James C. Bathurst

arch 10, 1882
James Bathurst were also a China-man. Sam Wooley dressed out as a Negro Comedian. W. H. Dixon had a different take on that and came as Old Darkey. J.H. Paddock were a Big Clown. Joe Meyers dressed as a Soldier, but I figure he ain't got no more imagin-ation than me and just put on his old uniform. Same with Frank Roberts who came as a Sailor Boy. Oscar Bookholtz were a Song and Dance Darkey.

November 18, 1882
James Bathurst now in charge at Jim and Charley's Saloon.

November 19, 1882
Bathurst, feller tending bar at the place next to Devereaux's, had 3 men come in trying to sell him 2 cadies of tobacco. Bathurst didn't buy, as'n he thought some-thing weren't right. Instead, he tolt the Marshal about the 3. Marshal tolt Bathurst a rail car were stole from the night before, and them 3 might be the ones, so Bathurst, being a good feller, found them men and says he want to bargain. Marshal says he be near to watch. Them boys weren't stupid, and smelt a rat. They took off for the hills, but Stingley and
Sheriff Mix headed 'em off and tossed 'em all in the cooler. They ain't give names, but one knowed as 'Broken-nose Scotty.' Police-man Modie found 2 cadies of tobacco hid in a rail car the next day.

May 30, 1883
Marshal Stingley, Deputy James Bathurst, and 2 other fellers got gunned down in day-light. I seen it.
Thomas Ninemeyer, a charcoal burner from Brown's Canyon, what works for Millan and McKee, came to town with his father, his brother, Boon, Bill O'Brien, and Tom Evans. They was serious drunk and making violent threats all around. The Marshal and the Deputy took their guns cuz re-volvers and drunks don't make for good company.
Come 6 in the evening, them boys were drunker and was eating dinner at Bender's Hotel. Evans were full of Bender's rot gut, and got to being abusive to the cook and the waiters, and took to yelling for coffee. John Thayer, a rail-road man, told the waiter
girls to get out of the way and he'd wait on Evans, which he did.
He were taking his seat when the Marshal and Deputy walked in. That's all it took as'n the situation seems like it were a set up.
Ninemeyer, who ain't said a thing all this time, goes for his re-volver right away. He took to shooting while backing to the door. Evans went at the Marshal with a big knife. He got shot by Deputy Bathurst, and staggered out-side, and died on the side-walk not long after. An old

feller, name Gannon, black-smith for the rail-road, were sitting at a table minding his business. He stood up to get out of the fight and Ninemeyer blasted him in the chest.

Bathurst got shot in the left breast, just below the heart. He ain't likely to survive, the doc says, but he fighting hard.

June 7, 1883

Thomas Ninemeyer, cock-sucker what murdered Deputy Bathurst, Billy Brown, and that black-smith Gannon, on May 30, were brought back to town for what they calls a pre-liminary investigation. He been kept at the county jail in Buena Vista for his health.

September 6, 1883

Theys selling photo-graphs of James Bathurst, deputy what got murdered in May. Raising cash money for his wife and child who surely need it.

Joe J. Bender

November 16, 1880
    Bender moved his saloon from G Street to First Street. Good move, as'n fellers don't wanna walk way the hell over to G Street just to get drunk. Not when theys so many other choices closer to town.

November 22, 1880
    Bender had him a wagon parked behind his place and someone stole from it.

January 6, 1881
    J.J. Bender opened a boarding house and saloon over on the east side of First Street.

February 8, 1881
    Bender says a bunch of blankets gone missing. Can't says I blame who-ever stole 'em as it's colder and a miser's heart these days.

February 16, 1881
    Man named Gray got accused of stealing those hides what went missing from Craig's. The constable searched his house. Besides the hides, he found Hawkins saw, Joe Bender's comforters, and some rubber boots and shoes, all hid under the floors. Can't trust no-one, it seems.

April 17, 1881
    Town got a sight more exciting of late. Had us two fights this week. one were bloody but not serious. Mat Sheridan, a laborer on the grade at the depot, had a dispute with some feller in front of Bender's Saloon. This stranger gave Sheridan a whack on the back of the head with a Barlow knife and opened up a cut a few inches long. Stranger got throwed in the calaboose. He were down-right drunk which ain't no surprise. Need to put such fellers to work cleaning up the streets.

May 22, 1881
    Bender bought a house and the lot he's been using. Gonna add on to his hotel.

June 5, 1881
    Bender nearly thru building his two-story lodge.

June 18, 1881
    Bender roofed his new building in tin and Bateman supervised. After, Bender had a big ole party what 50 people joined. Cake and nuts

and ice cream served at mid-night and brother I ate my share and a bit more.

July 2, 1881
J.J. Bender, what owns Bender Hotel, damn near lost his mind. Had a customer at his restaurant what owed Bender $four.90 cash money, and that ain't no small amount. The man wouldn't pay up, so Bender follows the man into the street, near the corner of F and First, and pulls a knife and cut the feller across the ribs. It weren't a deep cut, but Bender did cut him.

Deputy Marshal Ruefly arrested Bender and took him to Marshal Taylor. Taylor took Bender to Judge Hawkins, but it were late by then and the Judge tells Taylor to bring Bender back in the morning. Now the calaboose were full, and Bender owns a business in town, he be some-one we all know, especially the Marshal, so he got turned loose for the night after promising to go to the Judge first thing in the morning. Bender ain't to be found next morning. Most likely went to Bonanza to hide.

That feller what got wounded swore out a warrant against Bender, and the law went looking for him.

After a few days, Bender made it back to Salida. The Judge had to turn him loose on account of the man what got wounded left town.

Story on the street is Bender's friends spent the last week convincing the man to move on down the line. Bigger story is, the Marshal knowed what they was doing and said nothing.

September 16, 1881
Bender adding on to his hotel. Gonna be two stories high with 15-20 rooms, the biggest in town. Joe Bender getting his-self rich.

October 12, 1881
Joe Bender digging a cellar under his hotel and using the dirt to grade First Street. Makes the road a bit rough for now, but will be better as it gets packed down.

October 23, 1881
Robert Murray, from Nova Scotia, what work in Duffy's camp on the Calumet iron mine branch of the Denver and Rio Grande, got kicked by a mule and his right leg got broke halfway betwixt the ankle and knee. He got brought to town to Bender's Hotel where Dr. Brown set his leg. Gonna be laid up a few weeks.

October 30, 1881
Bender's Hotel addition is done. City ordered him to clean up his side-walks as they be a mess.

November 26, 1881
   Stingley supervising men what be cleaning up in front of Bender's Hotel.

July 5, 1882
   Watched Joe Bender whack a feller in a fight at his place. Hit him right on the sconce.

May 30, 1883
   Marshal Stingley, Deputy James Bathurst, and 2 other fellers got gunned down in day-light. I seen it.
   Thomas Ninemeyer, a charcoal burner from Brown's Canyon, what works for Millan and McKee, came to town with his father, his brother, Boon, Bill O'Brien, and Tom Evans. They was serious drunk and making violent threats all around. The Marshal and the Deputy took their guns cuz re-volvers and drunks don't make for good company.
   Come 6 in the evening, them boys were drunker and was eating dinner at Bender's Hotel. Evans were full of Bender's rot gut, and got to being abusive to the cook and the waiters, and took to yelling for coffee. John Thayer, a rail-road man, told the waiter girls to get out of the way and he'd wait on Evans, which he did. He were taking his seat when the Marshal and Deputy walked in.
   That's all it took as'n the situation seems like it were a set up.

July 7, 1883
   Folks is mighty up-set with the Bender's on account of the murders took place in their place after they served liquor to them boys from Brown's Canyon. Theys a petition about to re-voke Joe Bender's liquor license. Mr. Shaw had a cooler head, and made a motion the matter be in-definitely post-poned, and the others agreed.

Captain Blake

June 8, 1880
Captain Blake, man what be the post-master in Cleora, done bought a place there and gonna move it here so's we can have a proper post office soon.

June 14, 1880
Theys started building Captain Blake's place for a post office, over on First Street and F. Gonna live in a house there while's a proper office gets built.

June 16, 1880
Captain Blake's building took a tumble. It weren't well built and a good breeze knocked it flat over.

July 19, 1880
Captain Blake planning on bringing his family from Kansas City soon as his house finished.

June 16, 1881
Captain Blake got his jaw in a sling since he come back from White Pine. Ain't heard why.

October 23, 1881
Captain Blake's wife died in Kansas City. They got 5 children, the oldest around 13.

October 30, 1881
Captain Blake heading back to Salida now that he buried his wife in Kansas City.

January 10, 1882
Captain Blake left for Kansas City. Not sure why.

John T. Blake

July 17, 1880
   Blake got him one fancy side-walk out-side his building.

August 7, 1880
   After a bit of shaking out, seems we settled on a few businesses for grocers—Web and Corbin, Meyer and Dale, W.W. Wilson, Frame and Company, Blake and Company, White and Company, Mulvany, M.C. Brown, and J.J. Harris.

November 11, 1880
   Blake and Company seems to be the only place in town to buy a proper Stetson hat if'n a feller wanted a fancy head-piece like that, but less you courting for a full-time, live-in woman I don't see the need.

November 17, 1880
   Thiefs broke into Blake's place and stole a comforter, three blankets, and a pair of pants.

December 10, 1880
   The grocery business too crowded here in Salida. Ben White closing up his store, gonna sell hard-ware, instead. Same with Blake. He gonna sell furnishings once he gets rid of his grocery stock.

January 1, 1881
   John Blake sells dry goods and had 600 acres here where part of the city got built. He put up one of the first houses in town on the corner of First and F.

January 2, 1881
   Three dry goods stores made it thru to the new year. Craig and Sanders, J.P. and George Smith (what started in Cleora), and John T. Blake.

April 8, 1881
   Our elections, such as they was, got W.A. Hawkins for mayor over Blake 50-48.

July 28, 1881
   Town folk having a big ole meeting over at Hunt's building to talk about pushing Salida as home for the State capital. Judge Hawkins gonna be there, along with the Craig brothers, Blake, French, Bateman, Smith, Devereux, Hartzell, Howell, Webb and Corbin, Israel, Galbraith, the Wilsons, Roller, Twitchell, and a few others.

January 3, 1882
Mr. Blake adding to the rear of his store with a front on F Street. 18 by 24 feet. Post office moving there.

March 19, 1882
Folks saying Salida need to buy the town ditch what now owned by Kelsey, Haskell and Blake. Sounds right. We need control over what happens here.

March 24, 1882
Up F Street, in the old post office stand, in the rear of Blake's dry good store, be a place opened by new fellers, Hively and Young. Theys gonna sell hard-ware, tin-ware, stoves, cutlery, lamps, chandeliers, and all that fancy kind of crap.

April 3, 1882
A new addition been laid out on the south-east edge of town. This one done by Blake, Hodgman, and Westerfield. Gonna plat out streets running square with the world, not following the rail-road like the first. They says they to have 2 or 3 broad avenues and 4 rows of trees between them. They plans to make it the finest in town.

April 5, 1882
F Street looking to be the place for business. Blake thinking of turning his store so's it facing F Street, right next to Hively, Young and Company. If he do, he gonna add a two-story brick building where there now be wood frame.

April 23, 1882
Blake contracted with W.C. Richardson to build a store-room next to the post office. Gonna be 20 feet by 40 feet, but only 1 story. Gonna be for the post office to move in so's they have more room. Salida getting so big the mail now bursting out.

April 28, 1882
Town board says 'yes' to getting water from Haskell, Kelsey, White, and Blake. $35 each month.

Judge J.B. Bowne

January 4, 1882
J.B. Bowne elected police magistrate by town board.

February 6, 1882
    Levi Graham and Ben Nichols, 2 colored fellers over at the Junction House, had a little round-up early Sunday morning. Graham gave Nichols a tongue-lashing, calling him some fighting names right in front of folks. Vile and ugly names they be. Graham got took before Justice Bowne and plead guilty to swearing but says he ain't done no fighting. Theys had a trial and Graham got fined $10. Nichols got hisself arrested for throwing dishes and pounding on Graham. Got him $5 fine.

April 11, 1882
    Max Dickman got a new safe in his lumber office. Only took him and his clerks a half day to open it. The boys was laughing hard at that one when Dickmans says A.T. Ryan and Judge Bowne was the ones what couldn't get the dang thing open. Ain't heard Ryan and the judge's take on the matter.

April 14, 1882
    We ain't all that high-class just yet. Feller name Pierce got hisself arrested for licking a woman. I shit you not. And she weren't even a whore. Judge Bowne fined him $10 cash money, but as'n Pierce ain't got no funds he went to work for the city.

May 4, 1882
    I'm thinking it near about time to light out for other parts. Another damn bunch of law-yers in town. J.R. Kennemur from Nathrop and S.W. Taylor partnered up. Opening in Judge Bowne's building, the one last used for White Brothers Meat Market. Seems to me a meat market is right proper for legal men. They sees every-one as cattle for slaughtering.

May 14, 1882
    John Kelly, a common loafer and scalawag, stole shirts from a clothes-line near the river. Judge Bowne tracked him down, throwed him in the calaboose, and fine the feller $10. Loafer ain't got no money, so's he working in the streets.

May 29, 1882
    Charles Phillips were before Judge Bowne on drunk and disorderly. $5 fine.

June 21, 1882
    John Kelley were drunk and disorderly. Got lodged in the calaboose before Judge Bowne fined him $5. He ain't got no money, so's they put a ball and chain on his foot and put him to work. Kelley he ain't liked that none at all. Picked up the ball, went down to the bridge, and jumped off, landing on a island. Hid his-self in the brush. Police-man Modie found him. Now Kelley ain't working. He just sitting in jail with no-thing but bread and water.

July 19, 1882
    Ain't no-thing do my body better than watching law-yers lose their cool. Had a case in Justice Bowne's court. Mayor Wilson represented Wilson Brothers. Mrs. Jennie Wells were de-fendant. Theys asked to move things to Justice Garrison's court. While Bowne were making out the papers, an altercation of words
broke out betwixt Wilson and Mrs. Wells law-yer, Mr. Starbird.
Bowne kept 'em quiet a bit, but things split on-to the side-walk. Them 2 air-bags engaged in enough words to fill a number of books. If'n words be blows them 2 would have filt the streets with blood,
but as it were they ain't done no-thing but suck air from the rest of us.

July 25, 1883
    I dang near wet my trousers laughing to-day. Stranger walked in-to Judge Bowne's, on the corner by Pomeroy's office, and asked where the Presbyterian church were. Judge scratched his head. It were obvious he ain't knowed. He turned to Jack Williams and asked him. Jack says he ain't knowed either. I ain't questioning the morals of either fellers, but even a drunk like me knows where the only church in town located.

Ernest Christison

April 11, 1882
Jesse Stingley, the Marshal's brother, married Miss Nettie M. Cameron at the home of her father, Thomas Cameron. The Naylor's was there, the Coffey's, the Reeds with their daughter, Miss Cameron's parents and brother and sister, Baxter Stingley, of course, and Ernest Christison. That last one odd, as'n he one of the fellers Baxter Stingley help run out of the valley back in the Lake County War days. Time heals all they says.

September 3, 1883
The cattle grower's convention were held in Poncha yester-day. I heard that talk got around to the Watkins lynching for cattle thieving. Seems theys a gang been working Chaffee County for some time, and they stoled over $200,000 of cattle. Says it started with only a hand-ful here and there, but as they ain't been caught nor punished, this gang now running off entire bunches, horses too. 60-70 head at a time.

July 6, Ernest Christison, local boy I wrote on, got his-self arrested up to South Park with 4 others. They changed some brands but were sloppy with it, and the old brands was easy to see.

October 28, 1883
Lord a mighty, Lord a mighty, what terrible sad times. I shed my tears along with others. Marshal Baxter Stingley got shot down in cold blood. He dead.

Remember way back to the Lake County War days, and not so long ago to the cattle thief what were lynched? And that night Frank Reed backed Stingley off serving a warrant? All them birds come home to roost to-day.

Frank Reed done the murder. He part of that cattle-thieving bunch, with Edward Watkins and Ernest Christison and others. When not a thief he worked in Mix and Company's brick-yard. Ain't no one what weren't aware them boys stoled cows. Only no-one done no-thing about it, and now the Marshal be dead.

November 1, 1883
Ernest Christison in jail over to Buena Vista for his own safety. Sheriff Painter grabbed him first thing the next morning and held him under guard until the transport.

Edward Corbin

June 16, 1880
Couple of young fellers moved in from Cleora. Name Elias Webb and Edward Corbin. Gonna open a grocery. They bought three 30 foot lots from Chaffee County Bank, over on the west side of F Street, betwixt Front and First, so sounds like they be money men.

June 19, 1880
Webb and Corbin mean business. Theys busy on a two-story building on F Street right across from them news-paper fellers office, the one printing what he calls *The Mountain Mail*.

June 27, 1880
Webb and Corbin says they be open next week selling groceries.

July 20, 1880
Them Webb and Corbin fellers be making money hand over fist. Theys already putting a addition on their store.

September 23, 1880
Webb and Corbin adding upstairs to their building for boarders, and Mr. Webb sent for his family to join him in Salida. That be a sure sign this town ain't just a boom.

December 4, 1880
Webb and Corbin be go-getters. Traveling all over Gunnison and Chaffe County selling groceries to the new towns what pop up daily.

February 20, 1881
Edward Corbin's brother in town from Joliet, Illinois. Seems he's a grocery man also.

October 1, 1881
Edward Corbin and wife heading back East for at least 6 weeks.

March 5, 1882
Edward Corbin a go-getter. He setting up a pork packing company. Wonder how a feller gets a pig to agree to such?

April 2, 1882
Ole Corbin took to panning gold right from the dirt on F Street. Seen it with my own eyes. Says he gonna stake the town and run all the dirt through the mill.

April 28, 1883
    Webb, Corbin, and A.W. Jones bought 300 lots in town to build on and sell. They damn near own every-thing a man can see. Except my tent and I suspect theys want that too.

September 13, 1883
    Johnson and Chenoweth contracted with Edward Corbin, grocery feller, to build him a 2-story house, 7 room Mansard roof home.

L. W. Craig

September 12, 1880
Got us yet another dry goods store, Craig and Sanders.

October 18, 1880
Craig and Sanders got 100 blankets at their store and just in time.

October 24, 1880
W.A. Hawkins, R.B. Hallock, and L.W. Craig put up $75,000 in stock to start the Colorado Fire Brick Company.

January 1, 1881
Craig and Sanders still run a dry goods store. Came here in September. L.W. Craig be from St. Louis.

January 2, 1881
Three dry goods stores made it thru to the new year. Craig and Sanders, J.P. and George Smith (what started in Cleora), and John T. Blake.

January 16, 1881
Craig and Sanders closed. Yet another business gone under.

February 1, 1881
Two fellers got arrested for stealing hides from L.W. Craig and also the butcher shop. Gonna try 'em end of the week.

February 16, 1881
Man named Gray, not the one what run the hotel, got accused of stealing those hides what went missing from Craig's.

March 23, 1881
Appears Marshal Morgan might have taken a bunch of money before he lit out on the train, supposed to be chasing a bond but most likely running to safety. Owes quite a few bills here in town, especially to Bender, Craig, and Moll.

March 26, 1881
W.B. Pargood, stranger here-abouts, convinced Mr. Craig to loan him $14 before he went to Silver Creek. Showed Craig a note for $400 from A. Arbour. Told Craig he were a brother Mason and promised to repay. Of course, Pargood didn't repay and Craig had him arrested for petty larceny. The note were a forgery. Feller admitted he

done this scam a few times. Got him over to Buena Vista now, waiting trial.

April 2, 1881
    L.W. Craig took the pneumonia now

April 6, 1881
    I knowed some-thing weren't right with that Marshal Morgan. L.W. Craig got a letter to-day from Laramie, Wyoming what said Morgan got dis-charged from the Army over some trouble. Got his-self sent to prison there for stealing tents and were just released last spring.

April 8, 1881
    Our elections, such as they was, got W.A. Hawkins for mayor over Blake 50-48. French, Bateman, Craig, and Wilson trustees.

April 24, 1881
    Craig still ain't over the pneumonia. Gonna travel to Denver for a better doctor.

May 2, 1881
    Some stole 12-15 pounds of ice and two gunny- sacks from back of Craig's store. Craig says to keep the ice but return the gunny-sacks.

May 19, 1881
    Craig finally well and moving about again. That pneumonia were powerful tough.

June 6, 1881
    That man what swindled Craig of $14, name Pargood, got found guilty and got four months in prison in Canón City.

July 28, 1881
    Town folk having a big ole meeting over at Hunt's building to talk about pushing Salida as home for the State capital. Judge Hawkins gonna be there, along with the Craig brothers, Blake, French, Bateman, Smith, Devereux, Hartzell, Howell, Webb and Corbin, Israel, Galbraith, the Wilsons, Roller, Twitchell, and a few others.

August 5, 1881
    All this talk of Salida being State capital got fellers painting their buildings. Craig putting a new coat on his place.

December 28, 1881
Feller named Sam Sandusky come to town from Missouri, took him a job selling dry goods for Craig Brothers. Seems a friendly sort.

January 3, 1882
Other than businesses, lots other growing going on. Craig brothers adding to their store so's they can carry Queensware and wallpaper.

Janaury 6, 1882
L.W. Craig took off on a business-man's trip to St. Louis, Texas, and points east and south. Gonna be gone 5-7 weeks.

March 26, 1882
Elections coming again. Got 2 parties: Citizens and People's. On the Citizens ticket be O.V. Wilson for mayor, C.F. Gatliff clerk/recorder, M.M. French, L.W. Craig, J.A. Israel, and A.W. Jones trustee. On the People's ticket be E.H. Webb mayor, F.D. Howell clerk/recorder, J.A. Israel, A.W. Jones, R. Devereaux,
and W.E. Robertson trustee.

June 23, 1882
Salida barely escaped a disastrous conflagration the other night. This the third or fourth time we been so lucky. Around 10 at night, Sam Sandusky, feller what clerk for Craig Brothers and sleep in the back of their store, went out-side to the rear, as he do every night, to see if everything okay. He seen smoke rushing out the ware-house door which be dug out in the rear of the place. He
took to shouting and alarming, and folks come running. Damage from fire and water betwixt $500 and $1000.
Seems the fire weren't no accident but were malicious set. Someone dropped fire through the stove pipe, the one them little boys tossing rocks down. I think it were fire-crackers, as them boys took to tossing some around town instead of rocks of late. I knowed Mr. Craig chased a few of them little snot lickers away for just such doings.
They ain't had no insurance on the goods.

September 22, 1882
First National Bank of Salida coming. Roller, Webb, White, Craig and some others signed up.

November 2, 1882
Craig Brothers putting water pipes in their store.

Herman Dickman

May 23, 1881
   Mr. Dickman left his team in the street while in a store. It started to rain and his team don't like the rain none, so's they started looking for shelter. They went right thru the front door of the bank to get dry, and knocked out part of the door jamb and some bricks. Them horses caused the most excitement in town since the circus last summer. Can't say Dickman found it entertaining none.

August 5, 1881
   Dickman opening a lumber yard next to Ryan's livery stable. His son, Max, gonna run the place once he recovers from a broke arm. He got it snapped in two places.

September 7, 1881
   Dickman's lumber yard and Ryan's livery got enclosed for a corral.

October 12, 1881
   Herman Dickman been sick. Thought he would die, but seems to be improving.

April 29, 1882
   Henry and Max Dickman dis-solved their business, Dickman and Sons. Henry says he getting too old. Max gonna run things on his own going forward.

Max Dickman

November 19, 1881

Salida ain't got no hall for meetings and parties and such, but that gonna change. Max Dickman bought lots on the north-west corner of F Street and Second, and gonna start right away building a two-story place what be 40 feet by 80 feet. Lower rooms to have stores and the upper part will be a stage and the like.

January 6, 1882

Max Dickman went to Park County. Rumor were he got married. Max says it ain't so.

January 30, 1882

Dickman's Opera House got framing of the second story up. Gonna be a fine place and looking to open soon.

February 4, 1882

Max Dickman building a addition to his lumber office.

February 21, 1882

To-morrow gonna have a big ole ball for the fire-men at Dickman's Opera House. $1.50 a ticket theys charging. I could drink all night for that but a good party it sure to be. Guess'n tough choices be part of life, but I'm hoping theys have some free liquor in-side.

April 11, 1882

Max Dickman got a new safe in his lumber office. Only took him and his clerks a half day to open it. The boys was laughing hard at that one when Dickmans says A.T. Ryan and Judge Bowne was the ones what couldn't get the dang thing open. Ain't heard Ryan and the judge's take on the matter.

April 14, 1882

Salida soon be stepping in high cotton. The great violinist, Ede Remenyi, and his troupe, will perform at Dickman's Opera House on the 25th.

April 29, 1882

Henry and Max Dickman dis-solved their business, Dickman and Sons. Henry says he getting too old. Max gonna run things on his own going forward.

June 1, 1882

Max Dickman moving to a new office in his Opera House.

June 10, 1882
George Stingley, relative of the Marshal, in town from Missouri.
~
Max Dickman thinking of turning the Opera House in-to a hotel.

July 7, 1882
Don't this beat all? A madam what runs whores, name Lillian A. Browne, suing the managers of Knights of Pythias, including Max Dickman, J.W. Williams, O.V. Wilson. She asking for $20,000 on account of that group ain't let Browne attend their ball the other night cuz they says she ain't no decent nor respect-able person. Wonder if'n any of them fellers ever visited her girls?

August 23, 1882
Constable J.D. Lester had a round-up with Max Dickman over wages due. Lester were sued on his official bond. Dickman is on Lester's bond, and admitted he owed Lester some money, but proposed holding back until the law-suit were done. Lester went at him, and got arrested for assault and battery. $10 fine from Justice Garrison.

M.M. French

June 10, 1880
Feller name M.M. French putting in a fancy store on one and G, offering doctor drugs and paints and chemicals and brushes and perfumes. Lordy, next thing we be having school marms and dances.

April 8, 1881
Our elections, such as they was, got W.A. Hawkins for mayor over Blake 50-48. French, Bateman, Craig, and Wilson trustees.

July 28, 1881
Town folk having a big ole meeting over at Hunt's building to talk about pushing Salida as home for the State capital. Judge Hawkins gonna to be there, along with the Craig brothers, Blake, French, Bateman, Smith, Devereux, Hartzell, Howell, Webb and Corbin, Israel, Galbraith, the Wilsons, Roller, Twitchell, and a few others.

January 7, 1882
A drunk prowling around town the other night. Got booted out of French's drug store for trying to steal a hatchet.

March 26, 1882
Elections coming again. Got 2 parties: Citizens and People's. On the Citizens ticket be O.V. Wilson for mayor, C.F. Gatliff clerk/recorder, M.M. French, L.W. Craig, J.A. Israel, and A.W. Jones trustee. On the People's ticket be E.H. Webb mayor, F.D. Howell clerk/recorder, J.A. Israel, A.W. Jones, R. Devereaux,
and W.E. Robertson trustee.

Judge Garrison

February 13, 1882
John Welch and Charles T. Burgess the damn idiots what did the robbing. Got took before Judge Garrison and got $750 bonds each.

July 18, 1882
Tuesday night, Mr. Yoakum heard a noise about his chicken house. He investigated and saw what look to be a man. Yoakum let fly with his gun 2 or 3 times, and the what-ever it was fairly set the ground on fire to escape. Next morning, tracks made by a high-heeled boot were dis-covered. Justice Garrison says only cow-boys and darkies wear such, so seems one of them types was after Yoakum's chickens.

August 13, 1882
Constable J.D. Lester had a round-up with Max Dickman over wages due. Lester were sued on his official bond. Dickman is on Lester's bond, and admitted he owed Lester some money, but proposed holding back until the law-suit were done. Lester went at him, and got arrested for assault and battery. $10 fine from Justice Garrison.

August 20, 1883
Had a big meeting at the Opera House to express indignation at that Watkins lynching, and to pay respects to the murdered man. All the big whigs in town were there, and a good many ladies there too. It were civil, but folks mighty angry.

Judge Garrison called the meeting to order. Mr. McDevitt, Watkins lawy-yer, spoke and says the feller were a model citizen.

Reverend Hastings spoke, and says it were a deliberate, cold-blooded murder.

Judge Garrison talked, and says every-one know Mulock the biggest cattle thief in the county, and says he gonna put all his energies to finding the perpetrators of the dastardly act.

A few others had words, including Mr. North who says he seen Mulock and his men steal them cows from Watkins ranch.

W.J. Hartzell

January 30, 1881
    Hartzell and Johnson gonna compete against that China-man.

April 20, 1881
    Hartzell says he have bundles of water-melons within the month.

May 1, 1881
    Hartzell tangled with his bronco and lost. Ain't got no broken bones, tho. Hartezell that is. Horse be laughing.

May 10, 1881
    Hartzell's bronco bucked him off again. Not sure which one of 'em hardest of head.

June 16, 1881
    Train from back East came in with a wandering string band on board. W.J. Hartzell and Clarence Mackey corralled the band. Hartzell went to work on his back room, cleaning and making lemonade. Mackey went around town drumming up folks to listen. The tunes were supposed to stop at 11 at night, as'n the next day was the Sabbath, but folks having such good times no one left until way past mid-night. It were a good time for all, a pleasant relief from the recent gloom what got hold of town.

July 19, 1881
    Ain't many working men around, what with the rail-road and mines. Hartzell worried he won't have enough labor to harvest his oat crop.

July 28, 1881
    Town folk having a big ole meeting over at Hunt's building to talk about pushing Salida as home for the State capital. Judge Hawkins gonna be there, along with the Craig brothers, Blake, French, Bateman, Smith, Devereux, Hartzell, Howell, Webb and Corbin, Israel, Galbraith, the Wilsons, Roller, Twitchell, and a few others.

January 13, 1882
    Hartzell got lumber on the ground for a new building in back of his bank.

April 11, 1882
    F.S. and W.J. Hartzell bought the Bank of Salida from F.W. DeWalt. DeWalt going to Leadville to run his bank there. The Hartzell's

already own Custer County Bank in Silver Cliff. Seems they spreading it thin to me, but what I know of banking wouldn't fill a half-filled bucket.

September 4, 1882
I heard a troubling rumor for them what got money, which ain't me. Folks says the Bank of Salida gone broke. Doors opened Monday, but they ain't got no cash to pay out. W.J. Hartzell, manager, gone to Silver Cliff for cash. Tele-graphs says he be back Tuesday, but we shall see.

Governor Alexander Cameron Hunt

In 1861, Hunt were a U.S. Marshal in the Colorado Territory. But, we call him Governor Hunt, cause in 1867-69 the President of the USofA, Andrew Johnson his-self, made Hunt Territorial Governor of Colorado.

May 20, 1880
Governor Hunt be in charge, and he be a bossy one. He do like ordering folk around, but I guess that's his job, such as it is. They got stakes crissed and crossed and looking so confusing I'm near afraid to walk. Never seen no town being built. Look like ants if'n you kick their hill for fun, but with a lot of dust and the infernal sound of hammering day and night.

June 12, 1880
Governor Hunt building his-self a big ole place on H Street betwixt First Street and Front. I heard it will be 50 feet by 50 feet with office for the man upstairs and rooms down. Not sure if'n he gonna be living there or renting
it out.

August 18, 1880
That Governor Hunt feller made Salida his official head-quarters. Seems a decent enough type. Even loaning out his building so's the Presbyterians can have Sunday services.

August 31, 1880
Governor Hunt got his hands in everything. He brought up the Hawkins Hotel from Cleora and is adding it to the Grand View.

October 12, 1880
Governor Hunt donated two of his lots, on the northeast corner of F Street and 3rd Street for the Presbyterians to build a church.

February 5, 1882
Business feller dickering with Governor Hunt for the lots on the corner of E Street and First. Wanna build ém a two-story brick
and stone place.

February 25, 1882
Governor Hunt bringing a bunch of trees to town but asking for promises they be cared for proper. He sent trees over to

Alamosa, and they all died cuz ain't no-one give 'em water or some such. Sounds like some-thing people down there would do. Ain't no sense amongst ém.

March 11, 1882
Seem the question of where to put the mill been answered. Governor Hunt gave 5 acres on the upper end of the Milk Ranch, the one by George Williams Ranch. Theys got the machines there already. Lord, it a shame I ain't got no rich friends what give me land for free. But it ain't free. Any fool knows that no matter
what the paper-work says. Money changed hands some ways.

November 2, 1882
Governor Hunt donated a lot on the corner of F Street and First for the national bank. Ain't that some-thing? Damn money men getting free land and me living in a tent with a mule. Life ain't fair.

Sing Lee

September 6, 1880
China-man, name Sing Lee, moved this way from Silver Cliff. Setting his-self up a laundry.

November 22, 1880
That yellow bastard, Sing Lee, reported to have a genuine opium joint inside his laundry. Them soiled doves be his best customers, coming and going all hours.

March 22, 1881
Sing Lee be one boss runner even for a chink. Last Tuesday, a cow were fooling around his property and she caught a shirt on her horns and started running. Sing, he lit out like he was on fire, jumped a wood-pile by Fitnman's law office and ran past the Hawkins Hotel. Got his shirt back, he did.

May 6, 1881
That China-man, Sing Lee, lost all his savings in Denver at a gambling house. Them yellow bastards ain't go no control over their ways.

May 21, 1881
Sing Lee ain't got no luck but bad. China-man got robbed $three.25 last night. Says he carrying now on. A China-man with a revolver can't have no good ending.

March 16, 1882
Some smart aleck cut Sing Lee's laundry line. That ain't right. I ain't fond of them yellow fellers, but whacking away a man's business is plain ole hate-ful. Sing, he says he "must look little out maybe so I catch him next time." That kind of talk ain't good for no-thing. This town gonna blow up if'n a yellow man starts to
 beating on a white feller.

August 23, 1882
China-man, Sing Lee, headed to China to get his wife. Lordy, next they be making a bunch of yellow babies what be running all over the streets.

Jeff Modie

March 17, 1882
J.F. Welsh, laborer at the stone quarry below town, were in Salida Monday night and got on a tear. He threw big words at police-man Modie. Modie later arrested the feller for making his-self too familiar with some young ladies on the street. Welsh, fool he be, fought Modie and kicked up a deuce of a rumpus. Got his-self fined for drunk and disorderly when the judge heard about it.

April 18, 1882
Speaking of beatings, Assistant Marshal Modie got beat on when he were making rounds on Second Street near the Driftwood. Modie a tough one, tho. After the fight, he arrested Charles Rollinton and tossed him in jail. $35 fine. Loose woman name Anna Layton or Lawrence, I ain't sure which, got arrested for helping out, but judge turned her loose.

May 30, 1882
Police-man Jeff Modie back on duty, but ain't right yet from the bruises he got from that beating he took a few nights back.

May 15, 1882
John Roberts, a young man what been laying around saloons in town a few months, scraping funds to-gether as a roust-about and pretending to be a gambler, has had 2 or 3 bad breaks. Yester-day night he went too far. Marshal Stingley and police-man Modie went to take him in. Had to call him back with gun-shots when Roberts tried to run away. Got charged with carrying a concealed weapon and resisting arrest. He pled guilty. This the second time he charged with such, so's the Judge laid it on him and fined $50 plus court costs. Brother, that's some serious cash. Roberts ain't got such money, so's he joining the others on the road work crew.

June 15, 1882
Marshal Stingley and police-man Modie says a gang of confidence man in town. They says the gang best get to walking while the walking still good.

June 21, 1882
John Kelley were drunk and disorderly. Got lodged in the calaboose before Judge Bowne fined him $5. He ain't got no money, so's they put a ball and chain on his foot and put him to work. Kelley he ain't liked that none at all. Picked up the ball, went down to the bridge, and jumped off, landing on a island. Hid his-self in the brush. Police-man

Modie found him. Now Kelley ain't working. He just sitting in jail with no-thing but bread and water.

July 19, 1882
Monday evening a tele-graph came for Deputy Sheriff Mix from Under Sheriff Paint, in Buena Vista, what says to watch for and arrest a man what stole a horse up the river. Mix had police-man Modie look out after getting a description of the horse. Horse were found in Ryan's livery stable, and the man were found in a dance hall and locked up in the quay. Later that night, feller what claim to be a partner of the man locked up told Modie he knew the feller be innocent. Modie says, "Perhaps you are the man I want, so I'll put you in the cooler, too." When Modie asked the man his name, he says, "Do you want my Colorado name or my right name?" Says he called Terry. Officer from Lake County came down the next day and took the man back.

July 29, 1882
Burglars broke into Ruefly's jewelry store the other night and gobbled some of his tools. They broke the front window to get in. Police-man Modie found one of the work drawers near the Shirley house and some of the tools near the round-house. Ruefly lost $10-$15.

~
Police-man Modie says if the feller what held him up Sunday night come around he gonna whack him. It were near mid-night and Modie were meandering to the dance hall to see how things were going there when a feller jumped out, and yelled, "Hold up, there!" Jeff Modie belted the man with a right fist, knocking the man back 17 feet. Before Modie could get his gun out the feller were up and running fast as lightning.

November 18, 1882
There were 100 folks at the skate rink last night. 25 had on skates, and Police-man Jeff Modie were one. Hilarious it were watching him. One of his legs visited Pueblo, and the other went to Leadville.

November 19, 1882
Bathurst, feller tending bar at the place next to Devereaux's, had 3 men come in trying to sell him 2 cadies of tobacco. Bathurst didn't buy, as'n he thought some-thing weren't right. Instead, he tolt the Marshal about the 3. Marshal tolt Bathurst a rail car were stole from the night before, and them 3 might be the ones, so Bathurst, being a good feller, found them men and says he want to bargain. Marshal says he be near to watch. Them boys weren't stupid, and smelt a rat. They took off for the hills, but Stingley and Sheriff Mix headed 'em off and tossed 'em all in the cooler. They ain't give names, but one knowed as 'Broken-nose Scotty.' Police-man Modie found 2 cadies of tobacco hid in a rail car the next day.

G.D. Moll

October 26, 1880
I ain't one to spread rumors, but word be a smart man won't be letting J. Bendix have credit. Store owner G.D. Moll posted the same in the news-paper.

December 8, 1880
Mr. Moll dropped his revolver yester-day in his store and it went off. Luckily, nobody got hurt. Except for Moll's pride.

January 19, 1881
Seems our up-standing business-men might not be so up-standing after all. G.D. Moll is the true carrier of G.W. Gail and Ax Wares, but Twitchell and Roller been lately claiming the honor as theirs.

January 21, 1881
Well, if this ain't a turn. Walked by the new fire well the other day and folks be staring into the bottom at what look like a body. one feller, he dropped a big stone down the well and it sound like it hit flesh. G.D. Moll put on a six-shooter and got lowered into the well where he did find a body. Hauled it out and tossed the dead feller on the side of the road. Ain't no-one knowed who it was and that body lay there most of the day until some boys drugged it into a field and burned it. Weren't no Christian burial, just ashes and bones.

February 1, 1881
Moll has a box waiting at the post office, but he won't accept it. He put it up for sale. I think this be a big joke but time will tell.

February 4, 1881
That box Moll had for sale got bought by some tender-foot for 25 cents. Lord ain't there a sucker around the corner?

April 1, 1881
G.D. Moll had a kerfuffle with P.K. Vanvloten. They took it over to the field by the river and went several rounds. Can't rightly say if either of 'em won, but when the Marshal showed up both fellers told him it weren't a real fight. But it were.

April 15, 1881
John Elliott got shot in the head by Charles Roth, the barber. Kilt him dead it did. All over a woman.
These fellers was spun up over Mrs. McBriar, who gots a husband what stay in Bonanza, but Elliott and Roth both be calling on her.

Well, that don't never end up good, two fellers wooing the same girl and her with a husband to boot.

Tuesday, Elliott went over to Roth's shop to discuss the matter. They had a friendly drink while talking, but Elliott couldn't keep it friendly and told Roth he gonna kill him if'n Roth asked Mrs. McBriar to the dance. Which he did. Well, Elliott followed 'em to the party like a mountain lion, skulking around all night.

Round-about one in the morning, the couple snuck out the party and took the lower bridge home to avoid Elliott.

After dropping off the woman, Roth headed back for his shop, where he slept. He seen a feller near Mulvany's store, walking his way, and he got scared. Roth says Elliott told him he been warned about being kilt and Roth says he ran off begging Elliott not to shoot. While's running, Roth says he fired three times on account of being scared for his life. He kilt Elliott, then went to the Marshal and turned his-self in.

By that time, a crowd gathered. T.H. Reed and G.D. Moll were there. They put Elliott's body on the side-walk in front of Mulvany's store, then later moved it down to the New York House. Marshal ain't find no gun at all on Elliott.

Mr. Israel says Elliott tried to buy a revolver a few days earlier, but Israel didn't have a gun to sell. So, Elliott tried to buy one from Woolworth but couldn't get no credit. Few days after Woolworth turned him down, Elliott got arrested for breaking into Mrs. McBriar's millinery shop, but he weren't locked up cause he promised to stop all the trouble.

Coroner report got Judge Hawkins to issue a warrant and Roth he got arrested for murder. Going to trial soon.

April 16, 1881

Remember when Moll and P.K. Vanvloten had a round-up out at the field? Seems Vanvloten decided Salida ain't the place for him and moved down to Sedgwick.

He were a employee of Moll and the story be that Moll gave him credit to buy some goods for a new store in Sedgwick. Vanvloten went to Sedgwick and filed charges there,
claiming Moll stole from him. Truth be, Vanvloten returned the
goods to Moll first. Liar he be. Now I be a sight sorry I didn't help Moll whip his lying ass. But Moll handled it proper, like a man, and that be that.

July 1, 1881

Mr. Moll selling his goods at auction this week. Another business died.

July 18, 1881

Salida had a close call. Mr. Moll woke up before day-light and found his room full of smoke and his bed on fire. Says he can't account for the fire, but every-one knows he fell asleep with a cigar in his mouth. Damn fool lucky he ain't a crisp along with the whole town. Maybe Moll just distracted as he recent sold all his accounts to Mr. Roller and planning on leaving town. Being broke will make a man forget things.

October 11, 1881
Moll finally closed up and gone to Denver. I wish him well.

July 6, 1882
Remember G.D. Moll, feller what were agent of Gail and Ax, dealers in tobacco and cigars? He were one of the first enterprisers in Salida, always up to some-thing. He the one what fought 1 of his employees, and loved the attention he got for that in the news-paper on account of he seen it as free advertis-ing for his business. This the same feller what buckled up a gun and got lowered in-to the well when theys a dead body at the bottom. Well, he went over to Denver if'n you recall. Been on their police force a while, always in their news-paper for arresting bad men. Now he knowed for some-thing new. Moll got married to a lady name Pauline Peinders from Brooklyn, New York. That there is a pure act of bravery on his part, and I tips my hat to him.

M.R. Moore

June 5, 1880
The Mountain Mail prints first edition.

June 25, 1880
Talked to them paper fellers, M.R. Moore and H.C. Olney. Turns out the kerfuffle betwixt them and the Buena Vista news-paper fellers be over the rail-road. Seems folks up-river wanted it for their-self and figure folks here out-smarted 'em. If they'd see these damn fools arguing over why they ain't no bridge across the river yet. they wouldn't figure smart played no part.

March 15, 1882
Them news-paper fellers, Moore and Olney, dis-solved their partnership. Olney retiring, so Moore gonna be running the paper business by his lone-some.

October 19, 1882
That Moore feller, what edits *The Mountain Mail*, talked about the war. He a cripple with a damaged arm. Says he were a soldier for the north when it got shot up.

Henry C. Olney

June 5, 1880
    The Mountain Mail prints first edition.

June 25, 1880
    Talked to them paper fellers, M.R. Moore and H.C. Olney. Turns out the kerfuffle betwixt them and the Buena Vista news-paper fellers be over the rail-road. Seems folks up-river wanted it for their-self and figure folks here out-smarted 'em. If they'd see these damn fools arguing over why they ain't no bridge across the river yet. they wouldn't figure smart played no part.

March 15, 1882
    Them news-paper fellers, Moore and Olney, dis-solved their partnership. Olney retiring, so Moore gonna be running the paper business by his lone-some.

Dr. J.W. O'Connor

May 3, 1882
A new dentist, W.A. Smith, set to take in patients starting next week. Don't rightly see his place being in my path. He gonna office in the new small place Westerfield, built behind the real estate office on the corner of F Street and First. Dr. O'Connor to be there too.

July 26, 1882
Dr. O'Connor says the likely-hood of catching typhoid fever be high in the bottoms on the east side of the river if'n some -one don't clean up the dirty water and do some-thing about the stagnant water.

December 23, 1882
Betwixt 4 and 5 Sunday morning Dr. O'Connor got called to visit Kate Armstead's, colored woman what lives in a small house in the rear of the Grand View Hotel. When the doctor got there, Kate were un-conscious. Doctor says it were opium or morphine poisoning. He gave a anti-dote but it ain't worked. 3 that after-noon she were dead.

January 9, 1883
Rail brake-man, R. Gillip, had a awful accident around 3 p.m. Lost 3 fingers on his right hand. He were coupling a few loaded cars when a big wind come up, blowing smoke in from the coal kiln near-by. It were thick and blinded Gillip and he got his hand caught betwixt the bumper, smashing it to jelly. Theys brought him to Salida, to the Ogden House, where Dr. J.W. O'Connor cut off those 3 fingers. Doc used chloroform, but the feller still suffered greatly. He were a tough one to knock out.

September 23, 1883
I knowed I shouldn't have, but I damn near busted a gut laughing at a meeting last night over to the Opera House. Folks looked at me like I passed gas in church. What were it made me loose my manners? Theys organizing to build a gymnasium. What that be? A place for folks to do what they calls exercise. That's what money folk need cuz they don't do no proper work, getting their hands dirty and shirts sweaty. Ain't that some-thing? Theys even
elected officers. Ben DeRemer, president; E.E. Williams, vice president; Dr. O'Connor, secretary; Frank Crozer, treasurer. Gonna charge folks $5 a month, a month I says, to be a member. That on top of $2 just to get the right to pay $5 a month. Already got 50 folks signed up. I shit you not.

H.C. Pomeroy

May 3, 1882
Speaking of Westerfield, his new addition, the one he building with Blake, is coming up fast. J.A. Robertson and H.C. Pomeroy, both from Colorado Springs, bought lots. Robertson building a house there. He in town to open a transfer wagon on West's block. Pomeroy got him 2 lots and gonna run a restaurant and lunch-room.

May 11, 1882
Pomeroy, new feller from Colorado Springs, bought Westerfields' real estate agency.

June 6, 1882
H.C. Pomeroy opened a store for fruit, confections, and notions opposite the Opera House.

May 3, 1883
H.C. Pomeroy, feller running the fruit store, got appointed police magistrate.

June 7, 1883
Ninemeyer must got a bunch of money backing him cuz he had a team of law-yers on his side. Judge Rice of Leadville, Ellsworth and Miller of Buena Vista, McDevitt and Lawrence of Salida, and some others were on his side. Prosecuting were J.S. Painter and S.W. Taylor of Salida. Justice H.C. Pomeroy were presiding.

June 27, 1883
Thursday night, John O'Toole, white feller, and George Jones, colored boy, 2 gamblers from over at Del Norte, got into it over a card game. I heard Jones knowed as a bad one back home. But it were just words, and that were that.

Later, they met up in the office of the Virginia Hotel, Front Street and F, each with a gun and each wanting to have at it, and they did so with-out even a 'How do you do?' to the owner, Mr. Waysman.

O'Toole brought his gun down on Jones head and fired a shot what went right over Jones head. Jones jumped behind the office counter and O'Toole took cover across the room behind the stove. For a few minutes, them 2 had a game of bo-peep with the stove getting the worst of it. O'Toole took off up the stairs, firing one shot from the top, down at Jones.

I swear them boys put a dozen holes in that hotel, but not a damn one in each other.

Officer Stewart showed up and took both men in. Next morning, theys before police magistrate Pomeroy. O'Toole got fined for firing disturbing the peace, and making a im-proper display of a deadly weapon, and he got fined. Jones, that colored feller, were charged with disturbing the peace, and also got fined.

July 6, 1883

Ain't had near the drunk-ness this July 4. Police magistrate Pomeroy thinks the saloons were conspiring against him, says they watered down the drinks. Says he knowed 3 or 4 men what drank all day and got more sober. I weren't one of 'em. I woke with a power-ful head-ache.

August 14, 1883

At the town council meeting, Pomeroy got named police judge. That mean the magistrate office open. Theys gave Stingley a pay raise to $90 a month.

Septembe 25, 1883

This morning, Charles Ferritt filed a complaint against John Long, says Long stole $15 from him. Officer Stewart arrested Ferritt and, sure enough, found the cash on his person. Justice Pomeroy fined Ferrit $25 plus costs, and tossed him in the cooler until he pays. That ain't what you call a profitable transaction.

June 7, 1883

Ninemeyer must got a bunch of money backing him cuz he had a team of law-yers on his side. Judge Rice of Leadville, Ellsworth and Miller of Buena Vista, McDevitt and Lawrence of Salida, and some others were on his side. Prosecuting were J.S. Painter and S.W. Taylor of Salida. Justice H.C. Pomeroy were presiding.

William W. Roller

June 1, 1880
    Seems like some new fellers down from Cleora be expecting trouble. N.R. Twitchell and W.W. Roller setting up undertaker and furniture making business. Guess it's smart to not put all your eggs in a basket, but I'll be damned if I be working around dead folk, especially if I knowed how to make furniture. Guess them boys not be much for talking.

June 26, 1880
    I rode up the trail a bit the other day and watched that Roller feller dragging his building from Cleora for his undertaking and furniture-making business with Twitchell. He paid me a decent wage to help move big rocks and such, but mainly I was there so I could say I was.

August 19, 1880
    Them fellers, Roller and Twitchell, moved their tent back and is fixing to put that permanent building on their lot.

January 19, 1881
    Seems our up-standing business-men might not be so up-standing after all. G.W. Moll is the true carrier of G.W. Gail and Ax Wares, but Twitchell and Roller been lately claiming the honor as theirs.

June 9, 1881
    Lord a' mighty, Lord a' mighty what terrible sad times. I be a Christian man, but ain't never been one to pray out loud or nothing. But I saying plenty of prayers to-day. We had us a drowning. Little boy, five-year-old, name of Willie Roller, what belong to Mr and Mrs. W.W. Roller of that undertaker and furniture making business, got drowned in the river. He just disappeared in it. Bunch of folk ran to the river, up and down the bank, as far as Cleora but weren't no Willie.
    Willie and his brother, Arthur, and Eddie Mix were playing by the river bank. Some-how little Willie got his-self into the water.
    Seems them boys was trying to drink some water or dip a bucket and Willie slipped down the banks. The other two boys be
too upset to rightly give a account.
    They was two rail-road men on the opposite bank what went right into the water, but couldn't cross it in time to catch Willie on account of the current too strong.
    W.W. Wilson were there, and he tried but couldn't catch Willie neither. Wilson kept chasing for about a half mile, until he was by Scott's cabin, watching Willie's body pop up here and there. He lost sight of the poor little boy.

H.I. Wilson and A.T. Ryan, the livery-man, ran as fast as the Lord would let him to Bale's bridge, but never saw no body.

Mr. Roller and his partner, Mr. Twitchell, and about 30 of us looked for Willie until dark, and then eight men took lanterns and kept looking until mid-night. Folks started searching again come sun-up.

We knowed it ain't no use but we had to try. The river be up running fast, and muddy to boot. Willie so little and light his body might be caught under the water, on logs' r such, or the current might a taken it down-stream miles below.

Poor Mrs. Roller crazy with grief. Ain't never seen no man nor woman so upset in all my years. Breaks yore heart. They can't get her to eat nor drink. Poor woman overcome as'n this the second time she lost a child by accident. The youngest Roller child died a while back after being scaled. Such sadness for a family what seems to had a good life.

June 11, 1881

Lord a' mighty, Lord a' mighty. Such terrible sadness hanging over town. Still ain't found that Roller boy. Their family wrote this in *The Mountain Mail*.

A Card.

We desire to return our sincere thanks to the man kind friends who volunteered their services to search for the body of our little boy. It is a satisfaction to know that, although the search has thus far been fruitless, friends have done all that was in their power.

Mr. and Mrs. W.W. Roller, Salida

June 18, 1881

Still ain't found Willie Roller's body.

June 30, 1881

Lord a' mighty, Lord a' mighty. They found poor little Willie Roller's body, all the way down in Howard.

August 19, 1881

W.W. Roller now in the insurance business.

October 30, 1881

Roller and Twitchell added 50 feet to the rear of their furniture warehouse.

January 24, 1882

The big wheels in town about to get bigger. Webb, W.E. Robertson, Roller, and those Salida Mining and Milling Company boys to build a mill here to reduce low-grade ore from placer bars along the river. Gonna cost ém $10,000 and says to process 24 tons a day. Them boys gonna strip the sand right from the river.

February 3, 1882
    That Gold Nugget Placer Mining Company of Salida wrote what they calls a annual report. Got $500,000 and 50,000 share. Roller, C.T. Barton, and Twitchell be directors. That's a bunch of money, and not one of them dudes ever bothers to buy a round.

April 22, 1882
    It the week for parents. W.W. Roller's folks came from Kansas like the Stingley's. Don't know they knowed one another. Roller's papa heading to Gunnison County to look at mining property. I knowed Roller be from money. Ain't many working fellers getting rich in Salida.

May 4, 1882
    Twitchell, Roller, and Hodgman all gots a bunch of fruit trees and shrubs to plant around their homes. Next, they be having white picket fences and doilies on the table. Ain't much room left for working fellers what don't use the proper fork.

December 7, 1882
    Town board full of thieves in suits, that's for damn sure. They removed Roller as treasurer on account of he kept $650 what weren't his even after theys asked him for it. They says it were il-legal. Them money fellers ain't no-thing but robbers in suits.

January 2, 1883
    Roller and Twitchell dis-solved their partner-ship. Twitchell gonna sell real esate and insurance at the old building. He bought out Roller. Roller bought the furniture business back from Julius Ruff.

June 22, 1883
    Clara M. Roller, lady married to William W. Roller, thems what had the little boy drown? She died. Weren't but 31 years old. Folks saying a broken heart done it.

July 14, 1883
    One of them fraternities, called The Masons, had a planning meeting to form a lodge in Salida. Roller, Westerfield, J.H. Moody, A.F. Holland and the other money fellers were part of the group.

August 21, 1883
    Roller sold his furniture business to J. Witmaer and Company, who gonna keep running it a the same place on First Street. Roller spending his time with mining interests.

A.T. Ryan

July 15, 1880
Jones sold his livery to a man name Ryan.

October 19, 1880
Two horses what belong to the feller selling fruit and produce on Front Street got stole. A harness what belong to Mr. Higgins and a wagon in the yard at Ryan and Piper's livery stable got stole too. Thieves took off with a lot of bacon what were out front of Webb and Corbin's grocery. Parties went looking and found the wagon under some pinons on the west side of the river about five miles up. Weren't no thieves found but all the goods was there.

June 9, 1881
Lord a' mighty, Lord a' mighty what terrible sad times. I be a Christian man, but ain't never been one to pray out loud or nothing. But I saying plenty of prayers to-day. We had us a drowning. Little boy, five-year-old, name of Willie Roller, what belong to Mr and Mrs. W.W. Roller of that undertaker and furniture making business, got drowned in the river. He just disappeared in it. Bunch of folk ran to the river, up and down the bank, as far as Cleora but weren't no Willie.

Willie and his brother, Arthur, and Eddie Mix were playing by the river bank. Some-how little Willie got his-self into the water.

Seems them boys was trying to drink some water or dip a bucket and Willie slipped down the banks. The other two boys too upset to rightly give a account.

They was two rail-road men on the opposite bank what went right into the water, but couldn't cross it in time to catch Willie on account of the current too strong.

W.W. Wilson were there, and he tried but couldn't catch Willie neither. Wilson kept chasing for about a half-
mile, until he was by Scott's cabin, watching Willie's body pop up here and there. He lost sight of the poor little boy.

H.I. Wilson and A.T. Ryan, the livery-man, ran as fast as the Lord would let him to Bale's bridge, but never saw no body.

July 6, 1881
Last Sunday, a feller, S.W. Cox, came to town from Maysville and had him a bunch of mules he tried to sell for cheap. He told one man he traded a share of a mine for the mules and wanted what-ever he could get so's he could invest in another mine. He sold the mules to the livery-man, A.T. Ryan, for $75 which were special cheap even for a feller from Maysville. Weren't long until the real owner of the mules, man name G.W. Gruver, come looking for 'em. He had Cox arrested back in

Maysville and brought back to Salida to see Judge Hawkins. Cox sits in the county jail cuz he ain't got $500 bail and will sit there until the District Judge makes it back to these parts.

July 18, 1881

Salida's A.T. Ryan appointed Deputy Sheriff for this part of the county. Good choice. If'n Ryan gets after a man he gonna catch him.

August 3, 1881

Ryan bought the lot next to the livery stable so's he can build a bigger place.

August 24, 1881

Lordy, but we had us a round-up.

Big bunch of cow-boys made it to Salida, including Roe Cameron, Billey Taylor, Earnest Christison (feller what got runned outa the country in that Lake County War), Watkins, and a man I ain't never met. They all got drunk and started shooting in the streets. Even went so far as to hold up a man and his wife what just out walking near the upper bridge.

Later, Cameron came storming thru a few saloons, his revolver drawn and pointed, looking for Christison, screaming he would "shoot the damned son-of-a-bitch if I find him." Cameron then went into Heizer's butcher shop and fired a round. He held Heizer and started snapping his revolver in the man's face. Deputy Sheriff Ryan showed up, and with the help of a few fellers, grabbed Cameron by the collar and arrested him.

Cameron got out on bail the next day and Judge Hawkins fined him $50 after Cameron pled guilty.

Our fucking town Marshal hid the whole time. If not for Deputy Sheriff Ryan, there be dead bodies in the street that night for sure. Town fired the Marshal the next day. Cowards ought not
to put on a badge less'n they willing to earn their pay.

August 28, 1881

A.B. Taylor, the Marshal what just got the heave-ho, says he been treated unfairly. Taylor says when things got wild that night he asked for help from a bunch of fellers, on account of one man, even a law-man, can't get the drop on a group that large, especially when they drunk and shooting. Taylor says ain't no one but Uncle Dave Shobe offered to help him. Taylor also says that Billey Taylor the ring-leader of the gang, but Deputy Sheriff Ryan let him walk free that same night, and Judge Hawkins ain't fined Billey one cent on account of Billey ain't got no money. Taylor says he was heading over to Heizer's to arrest Cameron when Ryan beat him to it. Says he gots witnesses what say the same. All's I know isI ain't seen shit of the Marshal that night. But I sure seen them cow-boys.

August 29, 1881

We had us a heap of excitement Thursday night. Had us a genuine mob intent on stretching a man's neck for murder.

Wednesday night, Deputy Sheriff Ryan went up to the camp of Mears and took possession of a saloon being run by a feller named Charles 'Texas Red' Stone.

Seems a rail-road teamster, name Shorty McCarkey, got killt near Mother Power's den, over in Mears, around one in the morning. Had three holes in him, one right thru the heart. Shorty got asked over to Mother Power's for some free whiskey, the story goes, but that were just Stone's way of getting him alone to rob.

Well, them rail-road boys got it in their heads that this Stone feller done the killing, cause some-one says they seen Stone walking outa that gulch right after shots was heard. What I knowed of Stone wouldn't make that hard to believe, but thinking a thing and knowing it ain't but two different things.

Stone got on a east-bound train right after the shooting with a couple of whores, Mother Powers herself, and a whore from Buena Vista, named 'Cock-eyed Liz,' which do make things seem peculiar.

Thursday evening Sheriff Stafferd got a telegram from Maysville saying Stone was coming to Poncha by train and should be arrested for murder and taken to the county jail in Buena Vista. Sheriff did arrest Stone and got both of 'em on the regular train to Salida.

Next train to Poncha supposed to head to elsewhere, but

Hank Combs formed a mob to meet the train and the mob took over the engine by gun, forcing the operator to change the train orders so's it be going to Salida. This second train were right on the tail of the first one, the one with the Sheriff and Stone. Combs had him between 80-100 fellers on board.

The mob's train came in right after the regular train, and the mob were on the trail of the Sheriff and Stone, who headed to the Hawkins House for the night. The mob searched every room in the place, scaring women and timid men out of their wits. But weren't no pay-off. The Sheriff, who now had Deputy Ryan with him, took off with Stone by the back-door and headed to the Mix House. Hour later, theys headed to the Bale Ranch, out to Cleora, where they spent the night. They headed for Buena Vista come first light.

Well, the mob were down-right crazy for blood and stirred things up awful like. It got so out of control that the Sheriff had all the saloons and businesses in Salida close up. Sheriff also telegraphed Buena Vista for a militia what made it to Salida between 11 and midnight. By time that militia got to town, the mob done gone home and things were quiet.

January 16, 1882
Miles Mix took over for A.T. Ryan as deputy sheriff. Seems Ryan had enough of drunks and fools. Don't know what took him so long to find the trail.

March 18, 1882
Next day, Brooks jaw-boned all for what he owed. Went over to Ryan's livery and rented a team to take his show to Poncha. When he got back, the team were jaded, and the buggy damn near demolished. Ryan whacked Brooks over the head with a club and swore out a warrant for vagrancy and swindling. Brooks got more free lodging that night in the calaboose.

January 15, 1883
Those what weren't dancing at the ball got woke good when the fire alarm went off last night. There was bells, whistles, and pistol shots shouting a fire were going on.

We all ran in-to the road, and seen A.T. Ryan's Livery Stable burning, the one on First Street, north of the rail-road track. Ain't sure how it started, but seem some-one set it. A stable boy were sleeping in the office. Weren't long until the whole place were blazing.

The loco-motives did a good job waking the town. The new little fire-bell, the one in the hose tower, tried hard, but it just too small to be heard.

The hose company boys were on the spot fast, but the fire plugs was 800 feet away, near Mulvany's, so's they weren't much water pressure. Plus, the plug closest, the one by Ogden House, got left open so it won't freeze which made the pressure low, too.

Many of the fire boys had their Knights of Pythis uniforms on, and the fire damaged them so much they ain't use-ful no more. Ryan's building got lost, but them boys saved the one next to it. There was a furious wind blowing, making things even harder. Six horses got burned and a bunch of buggies.

It were power-ful cold, and some of them fire boys got fingers and ears and noses injured. Them boys was heros all. J.M. Buster stuck with the nozzle until he were covered in ice from head to foot. Had to be taken away by friends and cared for. Charlie Rose got hurt bad too. Craig, Webb, and the Wilson brothers fought hard as did a bunch others.

May 30, 1883
Marshal Stingley, Deputy James Bathurst, and 2 other fellers got gunned down in day-light

Thomas Ninemeyer, a charcoal burner from Brown's Canyon, what works for Millan and McKee, came to town with his father, his brother, Boon, Bill O'Brien, and Tom Evans. They was serious drunk and making violent threats all around. The Marshal and the Deputy took their guns cuz re-volvers and drunks don't make for good company.

Come 6 in the evening, them boys were drunker and was eating dinner at Bender's Hotel. Evans were full of Bender's rot gut, and got to being abusive to the cook and the waiters, and took to yelling for coffee. John Thayer, a rail-road man, told the waiter girls to get out of the way and he'd wait on Evans, which he did. He were taking his seat when the Marshal and Deputy walked in. That's all it took as'n the situation seems like it were a set up.

Ninemeyer, who ain't said a thing all this time, goes for his re-volver right away. He took to shooting while backing to the door. Evans went at the Marshal with a big knife. He got shot by Deputy Bathurst, and staggered out-side, and died on the side-walk not long after. An old feller, name Gannon, black-smith for the rail-road, were sitting at a table minding his business. He
stood up to get out of the fight and Ninemeyer blasted him in the chest.

Bathurst got shot in the left breast, just below the heart.
He ain't likely to survive, the doc says, but he fighting hard.

Stingley got shot in the left groin, the ball passing by his bladder before lodging under the skin on the back-side of his thigh. He also got shot on the left side, where his pocket watch were in his vest pocket. The watch were shot to smithereens, but it slowed the ball enough to save Stingley's life. Punctured a lung, but ain't kilt him.

Ninemeyer ain't waited to see how things shook out. He took off running west on First Street, towards Devereaux's. I seen Chris Laub and A.T. Ryan try to stop him, and they got shot at for their pains.

A bunch of us took off after Ninemeyer, cuz shooting law-men ain't tolerable no matter the cause or drunken-ness. He run
past Ryan's Livery Stable and Moody's Lumber Yard with 50 or 60 of us giving chase. Fellers had what-ever weapon they could grab on the fly, rifles and re-volvers and shot-guns and clubs and knives. Me, I had my re-volver and a knife I keeps handy. We fired and Ninemeyer re-turned the salute which scattered most of us. Talking tough and being tough ain't nearly the same.

Watching the show, a bit down the road, were William H. Brown, a teamster. He borrowed a gun and un-tied one of his horses and gave Ninemeyer a chase. He got with-in a few rods of Ninemeyer, who now were on the mesa north of the rail, not far from William Van Every's home. Ninemeyer, the son-of-a-bitch he be, turned and fired at Brown, killing the man. Then he tried to steal the horse. The horse turns out to be the toughest of the bunch, and ain't put no truck with getting stole. Horse slowed Ninemeyer enough for Ryan, William Goring, and Charlie Rose to catch up and capture the villan.

I ain't gotta tell you that lynching was in the air. Ain't no need for a jury trial on such. His guilt weren't no-thing to argue. Only problem were no man wanted to be the one to lead the crowd in such nefarious doings. Mayor Westerfield and others urged the fellers to let the law handle it proper so's a murder weren't on no-bodies soul. I reckon that were wise, but I sure wanted to see that sorry whore's son swing. I knowed a lot of fellers felt the same.

By 9 that night, Ninemeyer were in Judge Garrison's office, under protection, less'n liquid courage take over and the rope
handed out sentence by the boys. I heard that around 11, they
sneaked Ninemeyer by wagon to Buena Vista to the county jail.

June 4, 1883
A.T. Ryan says he seen it all, and Ninemeyer fired the last shot when he were by Van Every's potato cellar. When Ninemeyer tried to get on Brown's horse, Ryan says Charley Mullen shot at him, and that stopped it all. Mullen were only 25 or 30 feet away.

July 1, 1883
Theys put out the program for the July 4 festivities. Ain't a mother's son gonna sleep in that day. Things get started at sun-rise with a firing of guns. Then theys a meeting at the Opera House at 9:30 for a parade with A.T. Ryan the marshal of the day.

September 9, 1883
Just before 2 in the morning, Mr. Whitney seen flames coming out of A.T. Ryan's livery stable. He told police-man Stewart who gave alarm by rapid firing his pistol. Nearly right away, 4 fire-men were on it.

The fire ate through all the wood and hay like it were no-thing, and spread all over. Jack Hogset took to the horses and got them out, but got his-self serious burnt. Johnny Burns saved 2 horses and Mr. Jackson, a rail-road employee, got to his team, tho 1 horse got burnt bad. Them fire-man had 3 power-ful streams on it, and soon it were under control, but all were lost for Ryan.

October 12, 1883
Ryan opened his new livery stable.

Benjamin Baxter Stingley

1874
There were others taking turn at leading the ring, names what you'll read about here cause they become men to be reckoned with in Salida. Fellers like John Coon and Baxter Stingley (became a Marshal in Salida) and Jim Moore, Tom Reed (another Salida law-man) and Tom Ivy.

June 10, 1880
Remember that Baxter Stingley feller, one what be part of that Committee of Safety as a ring leader? Building his-self a house now right up near F and two.

August 18, 1880
M.C. Brown put Baxter Stingley in charge of his branch grocery in Sedgwick and the Kirber Camp.

November 10, 1880
Baxter Stingley and C.A. Hawkins gonna open a saloon and billiard hall in the Hawkins House addition to the Grand View Hotel.

November 23, 1880
With Marshal Meadows on the mend, town appointed Thomas H. Reed in his stead. Baxter Stingley stood in a few days before that.

December 13, 1880
C.A. Hawkins bought out Stingley in the billiard hall. Stingley gonna head after the boom in Poncha to run a saloon.

January 16, 1881
Thomas Reed got made constable after Baxter Stingley resigned. He say Reed is better suited for the job.

May 15, 1881
Baxter Stingley's back in town.

August 25, 1881
Baxter Stingley popped in from Junction City. He say theys growing fast there. Folks saying Stingley would make a good sheriff and he should run for office next election.

October 11, 1881
Baxter Stingley came thru after being in Clear Creek Gulch. He says politics the hot talk every-where.

October 30, 1881
    Baxter Stingley got appointed Deputy Marshal.

November 9, 1881
    Baxter Stingley got appointed Marshal after J.H. Stewart resigned.

November 15, 1881
    Marshal Stingley's brother got to town. Came in from Ottawa, Kansas and be working with the butchers, Cameron and Helzer.

November 26, 1881
    Stingley supervising men what be cleaning up in front of Bender's Hotel.

December 12, 1881
    A cow-boy from near Poncha Springs, name Richard Radcliff, was in Salida looking for fun and trouble. Found him a bit of both. He got liquored up, then took to shooting his gun in the street. Marshal Stingley took the man's gun. Right away, the drunk cow-boy tried to fight Stingley. That be a bad idea as Stingley
a tough one. Cow-boy got his-self tossed in the cooler.

December 14, 1881
    Roland Cameron and Baxter Stingley gonna take over Cameron and Company's Meat Market.

January 20, 1882
    Tele-graph came to Deputy Sheriff Mix asking him to arrest a feller name Ruddle. It came from George Taylor at Marshall Pass, says Ruddle wanted for theft. Marshal Stingley arrested Ruddle about 7 Sunday night and tossed him in the calaboose, but come
early morning Ruddle and a bunch others ain't there.
    Also missing were a man from Buena Vista, name Dooley. He got his-self locked up for abusing his wife and calling her all
the vulgar names in the calendar. Then he got after her with a knife before the law got called.
    About 5 in the morning, when Marshal Stingley were making final check on the calaboose before turning in for a few hours of rest after a long day and night, he sees the jail doors busted open wide and the prisoners all gone. That included Reddy, the one jugged for bruising that female friend of his at Lady Gay Saloon.
    The Marshal figured Dooley headed home which were true. Dooley told Marshal Stingley that Reddy and Ruddle busted open the door by prying off the iron strips. Says they told him he gots to run with them and he did.

Reddy were found by the Marshal in bed at the Lady Gay and got tossed back in the calaboose.

February 13, 1882
G.S. Huggins, what got a second-hand store, got broke in to Tuesday night by a couple of damn idiots.
These fools teared off 2 or 3 boards from the rear of Huggins building. They got in-side and helped them-selves to cigars, pencils, notions, re-volvers and guns, few hundred dollars worth. Who the hell steals pencils? Any-ways, these boys musta been
drunk cause theys busted out a front window when leaving. The noise woke Marshal Stingley, who was sleeping in his room up--stairs, the next building over. Stingley rushed down and caught one feller. Not long later, he caught up to the other and got back most of the stole goods. All except for a .45 Colt re-volver and 2 Sharpe's rifles. Sounds like they be another feller what didn't get caught.

March 6, 1882
Baxter Stingley back in town after a trip to Gunnison. He say he were treated mighty fine by them folk. Ain't never heard much about that town other than people be kind.

March 14, 1882
Marshal Stingley checking for trash in alleys and back yards, and it about time. A mess it were here. I ain't living in town, but I sure don't like the look and smell of folks tossing stuff out their
door. Good for the Marshal.

April 9, 1882
Marshal Stingley got his jail crews digging holes around town to plant trees, particularly around Alpine Park. He sure seem intent on sprucing up Salida.

April 11, 1882
Jesse Stingley, the Marshal's brother, married Miss Nettie M. Cameron at the home of her father, Thomas Cameron. The Naylor's was there, the Coffey's, the Reeds with their daughter, Miss Cameron's parents and brother and sister, Baxter Stingley,
of course, and Ernest Christison. That last one odd, as'n he one of the fellers Baxter Stingley help run out of the valley back in the Lake County War days. Time heals all they says.

April 22, 1882
Seen Baxter Stingley and his brother Jesse with their father. He came in from Kansas. Them boys ain't seen their papa in 17 years, and that be a mighty long time.

pril 27, 1882
Had us a killing of sorts. About 6 in the morning, Marshal Stingley got called from bed by Edward Streepy who says J.W. Cozad were lying near death. Cozad also says a man at the dance hall had Cozad's watch.

Marshal got his-self out of bed and went to town to check things out. He found Cozad in bed in a room he rented over the Clarendon Restaurant. Doc got called, but Cozad got worser and worser and died at 9 in the fore-noon.

Stingley found the feller what had Cozad's watch. He were too drunk to rightly say how he came to have it so's the Marshal tossed the man in jail. Sober, the feller says it were Streepy his-self what gave him the watch. Says it weren't stoled. A warrant were writ for Streepy and Deputy Sheriff Mix arrested him for thieving. He also arrested a dance hall girl name Curly.

Friends of Cozad says he got drugged and robbed of $300 cash money plus the watch. Turns out the watch belong to Marshal Stingley. It were loaned. Marshal tele-graphed Buena Vista for the coroner to come figure things out.

Cozad been working for Devereux in his saloon and were knowed to carry a big wad of money around. Free and care-less he were. Every-one knowed he got on a spree of late of late, spending here and there like it weren't no-thing. He left his job at 7 the night before and headed to his room as always. Poor feller ain't stepped out of that bed again.

Coroner ain't yet figured it all out 'cept to says he think it were poison.

May 15, 1882
John Roberts, a young man what been laying around saloons in town a few months, scraping funds to-gether as a roust-about and pretending to be a gambler, has had 2 or 3 bad breaks. Yester-day night he went too far. Marshal Stingley and police-man Modie went to take him in. Had to call him back with gun-shots when Roberts tried to run away. Got charged with carrying a concealed weapon and resisting arrest. He pled guilty. This the second time he charged with such, so's the Judge laid it on him and fined $50 plus court costs. Brother, that's some serious cash. Roberts ain't got such money, so's he joining the others on the road work crew.

November 19, 1882
Bathurst, feller tending bar at the place next to Devereaux's, had 3 men come in trying to sell him 2 cadies of tobacco. Bathurst didn't buy, as'n he thought some-thing weren't right. Instead, he tolt the Marshal about the 3. Marshal tolt Bathurst a rail car were stole from the night before, and them 3 might be the ones, so Bathurst, being a good feller,

found them men and says he want to bargain. Marshal says he be near to watch. Them boys weren't stupid, and smelt a rat. They took off for the hills, but Stingley and Sheriff Mix headed 'em off and tossed 'em all in the cooler. They ain't give names, but one knowed as 'Broken-nose Scotty.' Police-man Modie found 2 cadies of tobacco hid in a rail car the next day.

November 24, 1882
Party called on Cheap John Fri-day and bought a fine suit of clothes, paid with a check. John found were worth-less, but not until the feller were gone. He swore out a warrant, and Stingley found the man over to Cleora. He got the clothes back, and let the rascal skip.

November 25, 1882
Late Satur-day after-noon, when a freight train came in from the east, rail fellers seen a body of a murdered man laying near the track above Cleora. The news spread with great excite-ment. Mix and Stingley went to the depot, and found a party of men had gone down on a hand-car to bring back the body. What they found weren't no dead body but only a dead drunk.

May 30, 1883
If'n folks thought Salida got civil and dandy theys thinking different now. Had us a shoot-out likes of which I ain't never seen. I doubt folks ever for-get this one.

Marshal Stingley, Deputy James Bathurst, and 2 other fellers got gunned down in day-light. I seen it.

Thomas Ninemeyer, a charcoal burner from Brown's Canyon, what works for Millan and McKee, came to town with his father, his brother, Boon, Bill O'Brien, and Tom Evans. They was serious drunk and making violent threats all around. The Marshal and the Deputy took their guns cuz re-volvers and drunks don't make for good company.

Bathurst got shot in the left breast, just below the heart. He ain't likely to survive, the doc says, but he fighting hard.

Stingley got shot in the left groin, the ball passing by his bladder before lodging under the skin on the back-side of his thigh. He also got shot on the left side, where his pocket watch were in his vest pocket. The watch were shot to smithereens, but it slowed the ball enough to save Stingley's life. Punctured a lung, but ain't kilt him.

September 15, 1883
Guess I ain't gots to be too worried about Salida getting duded up just yet.

Yester-day morning, 2 well-known cow-boys, name Frank Reed and Bent Jamison, came to town armed to the teeth and parading it for all to see, up and down the streets.

Marshal Stingley were cool as a water-melon. He politely informed them fellers about the ordinance against carrying weapons in the city limits and asked them to lay their guns aside. They said they would.

Around 12 noon, they went toward the stable, the one in the rear of Mrs. Fleck's restaurant, to get their horses and leave town. By this time, a warrant were put in-to the Marshal's hands.

It were from the sheriff of Saguanche County and were for Bent Jamison who were under indictment there. Stingley grabbed up

his deputy, Mr. Frizelle, and rushed over before them cow-boys could ride out. Reed were already mounted, but Jamison were standing in the lot, near the stable door.

"Bent," the Marshal says, "I have a warrant for you." Stingley's hands was in the pockets of his hunting coat—one pocket had the warrant, the other a small pistol.

"I'll never be taken alive," Jamison says and draws a .45.

I was watching, and you could see Stingley twitch as he thought to shoot the feller. Weren't Stingley's first round-up facing a gun, and I reckon he ain't liked the idea of being slow to draw again. I seen Stingley look over his shoulder. He seen Reed with a Winchester, cocked and leveled at Stingley and Frizelle. One of them were gonna die for sure. Stingley a cool one, tho. He kept talking and walking slow toward Jamison, backing him to the door. But there weren't no edge to be had, so's Stingley left, run down the street for a shot-gun and some help. But them cow-boys was fast. Theys long gone time the Marshal re-turned.

October 28, 1883

Lord a mighty, Lord a mighty, what terrible sad times. I shed my tears along with others. Marshal Baxter Stingley got shot down in cold blood. He dead.

Remember way back to the Lake County War days, and not so long ago to the cattle thief what were lynched? And that night Frank Reed backed Stingley off serving a warrant? All them birds come home to roost to-day.

Frank Reed done the murder. He part of that cattle-thieving bunch, with Edward Watkins and Ernest Christison and others. When not a thief he worked in Mix and Company's brick-yard. Ain't no one what weren't aware them boys stoled cows. Only no-one done no-thing about it, and now the Marshal be dead.

Reed bragged he won't never get taken alive for his crimes, and seems his word true as'n he gone from town, and Stingley's dead.

At 8:30 to-night, Stingley went in-to Arbour's Variety and Dance Hall. Baxter seen a writer for the news-paper and had a few words. Baxter then seen Reed and turned right, and walked straight up to the man cuz Reed gots a warrant for his arrest. Reed were talking to a bar-keep.

Stingley always had 2 guns, fine ones. He carried 1 with a bull-dog pattern, ivory handle and blue steel barrel. The other were a Colt .45, silver-plated. Stingley pulled the bull-dog one with his left hand, and spoke to Reed. I gonna remember them words the rest of my days.

"Frank, I have a warrant for you, throw up your hands."

Them boys knowed one another through Edward Watkins, lynched feller who were a firm friend of Stingley. Lots of folks ain't knowed they shared a house at one point. Watkins and Stingley was so close that when Stingley heard of the lynching, he headed straight back from Texas, where he were on a business matter, and swore vengeance. I don't know if Reed were one of those Stingley had in mind.

Usually a sound thinker, Stingley, showed poor judgment in the matter with Reed. Instead of standing a few feet off, with Reed covered by his gun, Stingley put the barrel of the gun against Reed's side. If'n he'd shoved the muzzle in-to Reed's ribs, he mighta been good. But he weren't. Remember it were only last month when Reed got the advantage on Stingley, forcing him to back down, and my thinking is that stuck in his craw, hurting is pride.

Frank were standing with his hands in his coat pocket. He yanked his hands out of his pockets and, quick as lightning, grabbed Stingley's gun away, covering the Marshal with his own weapon. They stared a few seconds, then Stingley went for his other gun, and Reed fired. He fired again and Stingley fired back. Reed then took off for the door, turned, and fired once more as Stingley chased after.

When Reed run out the door, the Marshal stopped running, which ain't like him. I got sick to my stomach cuz I knowed ain't but one thing make a man like Baxter Stingley give up the chase. He were shot bad.

Mr. Arbour and that news-paper feller called out, asking if he were shot.

"Yes," Stingley said, his legs all wobbly. "He shot me 3 times."

A bunch of us, and Mr. Arbour, grabbed Stingley and laid him out on a table. We took off his boots for comfort, and both was filled up with blood. A god-awful mess it were. Mr. Arbour says to move the Marshal to a private room and we done just that.

Dr. Underhill were there by then and he took over. The Marshal had 3 separate gun-shot wounds. 1 were through the right thigh. 1 were through the left arm. The last 1 were about 2 inches below his left nipple. Doc says Stingley got shot in what they call a artery, some-thing what carry all the blood, and he were done for. The Marshal ain't had a chance to survive.

He were only 38-years-old.

Nathan R. Twitchell

June 1, 1880
Seems like some new fellers down from Cleora be expecting trouble. N.R. Twitchell and W.W. Roller setting up undertaker and furniture making business. Guess it's smart to not put all your eggs in a basket, but I'll be damned if I be working around dead folk, especially if I knowed how to make furniture. Guess them boys not be much for talking.

August 19, 1880
Them fellers, Roller and Twitchell, moved their tent back and is fixing to put that permanent building on their lot.

January 19, 1881
Seems our up-standing business-men might not be so up-standing after all. G.W. Moll is the true carrier of G.W. Gail and Ax Wares, but Twitchell and Roller been lately claiming the honor as theirs.

January 20, 1881
Had us eight inches of snow last night. Mr. Twitchell were out being a ladies man. Had him a sleigh filled with eight women-folk, but damn if he ain't tipped it over and right in front of his own store. Them horses kept going like nothing happened.

March 4, 1881
Liquor won again. Twitchell got so drunk the other night at the party he proposed to two women. Worse, both of 'em said 'Yes', and he spent the rest of the night in a serious gloom.

March 27, 1881
Twitchell down with pneumonia but seems likely to recover.

May 6, 1881
Nathan Twitchell finally did it. Got his-self married to Nellie L. Fowle over at Colorado Springs.

May 18, 1881
Roller and Twitchell are big business-men. They own part of a mine over to Silver Cliff and word be they struck it rich.

June 9, 1881
Mr. Roller and his partner, Mr. Twitchell, and about 30 of us looked for Willie until dark, and then eight men took lanterns and kept looking until mid-night. Folks started searching again come sun-up.

July 28, 1881
Town folk having a big ole meeting over at Hunt's building to talk about pushing Salida as home for the State capital. Judge Hawkins gonna to be there, along with the Craig brothers, Blake, French, Bateman, Smith, Devereux, Hartzell, Howell, Webb and Corbin, Israel, Galbraith, the Wilsons, Roller, Twitchell, and a few others. Folks be dead serious about making Salida the State capital, and it do make some sense, what with the rail-road being based here and us in the center of the State.

September 14, 1881
Twitchell sure be a go-getter. He now a notary.

September 16, 1881
Roller and Twitchell now selling real estate and insurance. Their lots be $10-$100, over on E, F, and G Streets.

October 30, 1881
Roller and Twitchell added 50 feet to the rear of their furniture warehouse.

Elias Webb

June 16, 1880
Couple of young fellers moved in from Cleora. Name Elias Webb and Edward Corbin. Gonna open a grocery. They bought three 30 foot lots from Chaffee County Bank, over on the west side of F Street, betwixt Front and First, so sounds like they be money men.

June 19, 1880
Webb and Corbin mean business. Theys busy on a two-story building on F Street right across from them news-paper fellers office, the one printing what he calls *The Mountain Mail*.

June 27, 1880
Webb and Corbin says they be open next week selling groceries.

July 20, 1880
Them Webb and Corbin fellers be making money hand over fist. Theys already putting a addition on their store.

September 23, 1880
Webb and Corbin adding upstairs to their building for boarders, and Mr. Webb sent for his family to join him in Salida. That be a sure sign this town ain't just a boom.

November 23, 1880
E.H. Webb took the train to Denver to get his wife and babies. Theys all in Salida now and seem to be the happier for it.

December 4, 1880
Webb and Corbin be go-getters. Traveling all over Gunnison and Chaffe County selling groceries to the new towns what pop up daily.

January 15, 1881
Town got a official fire company organized. E.H. Webb elected foreman.

April 12, 1881
Webb stepped on his left eye Tuesday morning and had to tie it up with a rag. Before three o'clock 261 people asked him who he called a liar.

September 14, 1881
Webb got named chairman of the Republican county convention. He be a a good choice.

November 26, 1881
Webb ate so much Thanksgiving turkey he been sick ever since.

January 24, 1882
The big wheels in town about to get bigger. Webb, W.E. Robertson, Roller, and those Salida Mining and Milling Company boys to build a mill here to reduce low-grade ore from placer bars along the river. Gonna cost ém $10,000 and says to process 24 tons a day. Them boys gonna strip the sand right from the river.

March 26, 1882
Elections coming again. Got 2 parties: Citizens and People's. On the Citizens ticket be O.V. Wilson for mayor, C.F. Gatliff clerk/recorder, M.M. French, L.W. Craig, J.A. Israel, and A.W. Jones trustee. On the People's ticket be E.H. Webb mayor, F.D. Howell clerk/recorder, J.A. Israel, A.W. Jones, R. Devereaux,
and W.E. Robertson trustee.

March 30, 1882
I swear I shoulda learnt the grocery business. Webb, what part of Webb and Corbin Grocery, same feller running for mayor, bought 4 lots from Roller and Twitchel on the corner of Fifth Street and F. Putting a water line in it and planning a grand home. Even gonna have the plans on exhibit at his store in April. Ain't that uppity?

April 3, 1882
Election done. Wilson beat out Webb for mayor 198-158. Howell lost to Gatliff for clerk/recorder 195-118. Heard lots of false stories about Webb during the contest, but Webb kept quiet, thinking his reputation would take care of the lies. It ain't. Good
men all were elected, tho.

April 28, 1882
I swear the money men keep getting richer. Webb, Corbin, and A.W. Jones bought 300 lots in town to build on and sell. They
damn near own every-thing a man can see. Except my tent and I suspect theys want that too.

September 4, 1882
E.H. Webb running for State Senate at the county convention. Seem running a grocery ain't enough challenge.

December 10, 1882
Folks had a meeting at Judge Painters place to discuss a
library association. Webb got appointed chair-man.

ABOUT THE AUTHOR

Steven T. Chapman is a historian and owner of Salida Walking Tours and Buena Vista Walking Tours. He is a commissioner on the Salida Historic Preservation Commission.

The author of several fiction and non-fiction books, he is also an entrepreneur with multiple ongoing businesses.

For many years, he traveled full-time, living out of a Jeep and a tent, collecting experiences, stories, and friends. In addition to living in a dozen states in the U.S., he resided in Aruba, Canada, China, Indonesia, Malaysia, Mexico, the Philippines, Singapore, St. Thomas, and Thailand.

When not indulging his inner history-nerd, he is usually with Gina (a 2005 Jeep Wrangler) and his four-legged best friend, Rez (a 2018 Red Heeler/Basenji mix), exploring the mountains of Colorado.

ABOUT 'SALIDA SAM'

Other than his writings and a few notes from the original East-coast publisher, 'Salida Sam' Hayes is an unknown.

He claimed to be "younger than the mountains, but only by a few years," and never mentioned a birthplace. His only reference to home was one journal entry indicating he left in a hurry, possibly to avoid a warrant (or an angry woman).

'Salida Sam' often wrote about his experiences with a "full-time, live-in woman." She was a squaw he bought or traded for from a Ute chief, but their time together sounds short-lived. He never mentions what became of her only that "she couldn't cook for shit, but she did kick harder than any mule."

The only female Sam described fondly was Sue, his mule. He referred to her as "my one loyal companion in life, even if she does fart up a storm."

BIBLIOGRAPHY

BOOKS
- *100 Years in the Heart of the Rockies,* Cynthia Pasquale
- *A Brief History of Mt Princeton Hot Springs,* George C. Roche, III
- *A Colorado History,* Carl Ubbelohde
- *A History of Chaffee County,* June Shaputis & Suzanne Kelly
- *Chalk Creek to the Past,* Donald Smith
- *Chalk Creek, CO,* Louisa Ward
- *Colorado and Its People,* LeRoy R. Hafen
- *Colorado Citizen,* H.S. Lindbloom & J.T. Pottle
- *Down With Your Dust,* Ruby G. Williamson
- *Heart of the Rockies, A History of the Salida Area,* Kim Swift
- *History of Colorado, Volume II,* Wilbur Fiske Stone
- *History of the Arkansas Valley,* E.R. Emerson
- *History of the State of Colorado,* Frank Hall
- *Images of America, Salida Colorado,* Kay Marnon Danielson
- *No More Than Five in a Bed: Colorado Hotels in the Old Days,* Sandra Dallas
- *Nuggets From Chalk Creek,* Lacy Humbeutel
- *Our Spanish Southwest,* Lynn I. Perrigo
- *Portal Into the Past,* Clear Creek Canyon Historical Society
- *Rocky Mountain Mining Camps,* Duane A. Smith
- *Salida: The Early Years,* Eleanor Fry & Dick Dixon
- *Stampede to Timberline,* Muriel Sibell Wolle
- *The Charisma of Chalk Creek,* Stella Hosmer Bailey
- *The Killers of Judge Dyer,* Joseph V. Dodge
- *The Upper Arkansas, A Mountain River Valley,* Virginia McConnell Simmons
- *The Utes—A Forgotten People,* Wilson Rockwell
- *Trails Among the Columbine: The DandRG's Columnet Branch and The Turret Mining Area,* Dick Dixon
- *Transition from End of Track Construction Camp to Established Community,* David J. Ham

NEWSPAPERS
- *Aspen Evening Chronicle*
- *Buena Vista Democrat*
- *Buena Vista Herald*
- *Carbonate Chronicle*

- *Chaffee County Democrat*
- *Chaffee County Republican*
- *Colorado Daily Chieftain*
- *Colorado Republican*
- *Colorado Springs Gazette Telegraph*
- *Colorado Transcript*
- *Elk Mountain Pilot*
- *Fairplay Flume*
- *Gunnison Democrat*
- *Herald Democrat*
- *Leadville Daily Herald*
- *Montrose Daily Press*
- *Salida Daily Mail*
- *Steamboat Pilot*
- *The Denver Post*
- *The Mountain Mail*

MISCELLANEOUS

- *Sanborn Fire Insurance Map from Salida, Chaffee County, Colorado.* Sanborn Map Company, Sep, 1886.
- Stoner, J. J, and Beck & Pauli. *Bird's eye view of Salida, Chaffee County, Colorado.* Madison, Wis, 1882.

Walking Tours
Salida & Buena Vista

    See historic Salida through the eyes of a local on this intimate small group walking tour.

    Experience Salida's wild west past, history, culture, and architecture with a professional guide. Be captivated by fascinating tales of Salida's exciting, and sometimes violent, history. Visitors and residents alike come away with hidden secrets.

    Costumed guides lead this intimate, small-group walking tour. Be entranced by fascinating tales of Salida's remarkable history. Visitors and residents alike are amazed to learn the many hidden secrets of Colorado's largest National Historic District.

www.SalidaWalkingTours.com

Nonfiction by Steven T. Chapman

THE 'SALIDA SAM' HISTORICAL BOOK SERIES

Each book covers two years of Salida history, detailing nearly every fact, with rarely seen photographs and maps.

www.SalidaWalkingTours.com/shop

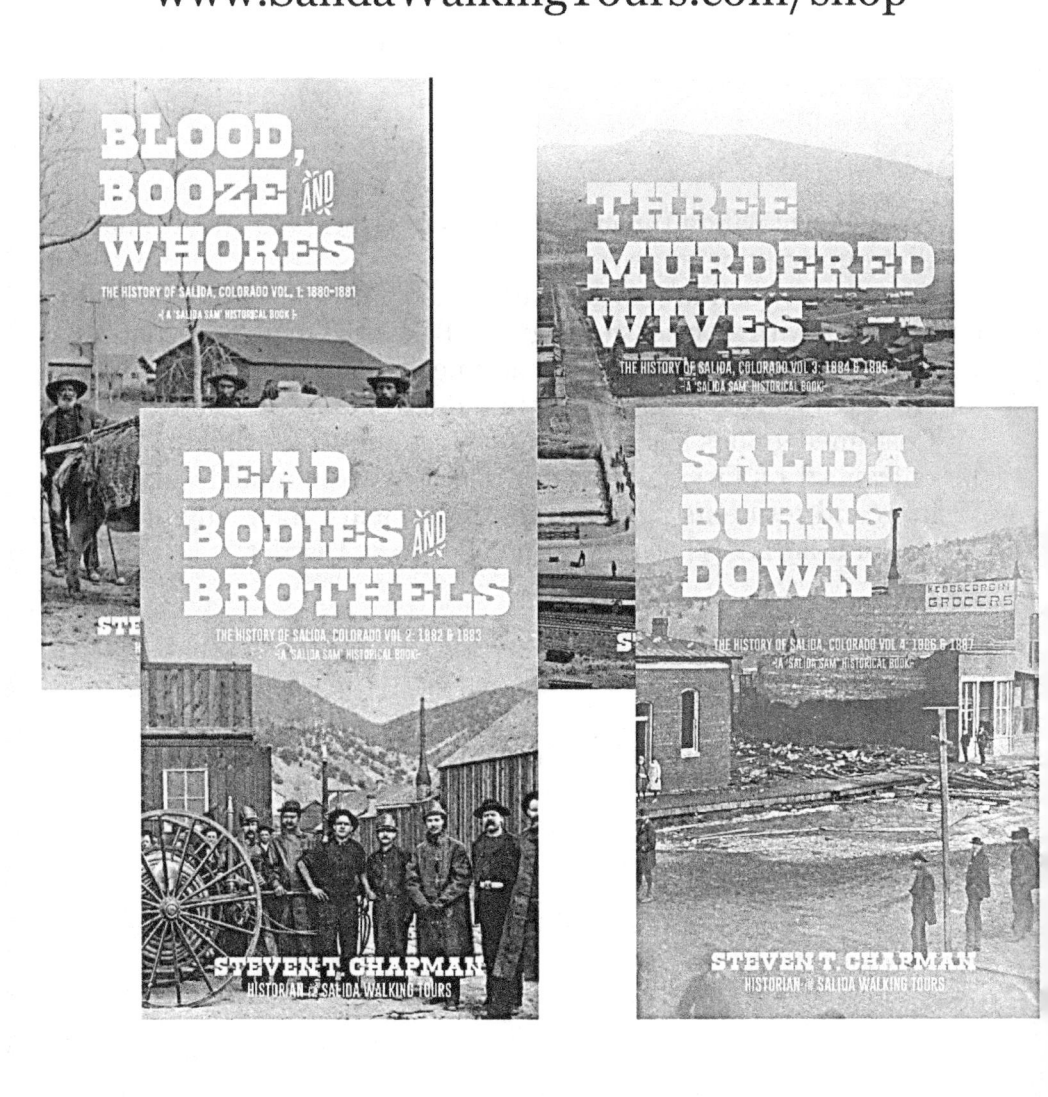

Nonfiction by Steven T. Chapman

THE SALIDA WALKING TOURS BIOGRAPHICAL SERIES

Each book covers the life and times of prominent, often notorious citizens of Salida, including photos, records, and details.

A Salida Walking Tours Historical Biography

MURDER!
The Criminal Conspiracy & Coverup Behind the Slaying of Salida's Most Famous Marshal

Steven T. Chapman

A Salida Walking Tours Historical Biography

LYNCHED!
Mob Justice & A Madness for Blood--The Vigilante Murder that Stained Salida for Decades

Steven T. Chapman

Fiction by Steven T. Chapman
www.StevenTChapman.com